1st EDITION

Perspectives on Modern World History

The Assassination of Osama bin Laden

1st EDITION

Perspectives on Modern World History

The Assassination of Osama bin Laden

Julia Garbus

Editor

GREENHAVEN PRESS
A part of Gale, Cengage Learning

GALE
CENGAGE Learning·

Farmington Hills, Mich • San Francisco • New York • Waterville, Maine
Meriden, Conn • Mason, Ohio • Chicago

GALE
CENGAGE Learning®

Patricia Coryell, *Vice President & Publisher, New Products & GVRL*
Douglas Dentino, *Manager, New Products*
Judy Galens, *Acquisitions Editor*

© 2015 Greenhaven Press, a part of Gale, Cengage Learning.

WCN: 01-100-101

Gale and Greenhaven Press are registered trademarks used herein under license.

For more information, contact:
Greenhaven Press
27500 Drake Rd.
Farmington Hills, MI 48331-3535
Or you can visit our Internet site at gale.cengage.com.

For product information and technology assistance, contact us at
Gale Customer Support, 1-800-877-4253.

For permission to use material from this text or product, submit all requests online at
www.cengage.com/permissions.

Further permissions questions can be e-mailed to permissionrequest@cengage.com.

Articles in Greenhaven Press anthologies are often edited for length to meet page requirements. In addition, original titles of these works are changed to clearly present the main thesis and to explicitly indicate the author's opinion. Every effort is made to ensure that Greenhaven Press accurately reflects the original intent of the authors. Every effort has been made to trace the owners of copyrighted material.

Cover images © Cal Vornberger/Alamy and © World History Archive/Alamy.

LIBRARY OF CONGRESS CATALOGING-IN-PUBLICATION DATA
The assassination of Osama bin Laden / Julia Garbus, book editor.
    pages cm. -- (Perspectives on modern world history)
    Includes bibliographical references and index.
    ISBN 978-0-7377-7306-4 (hardcover)
    1. Bin Laden, Osama, 1957-2011--Assassination. 2. Qaida (Organization) 3. United States. Navy. SEALs--History--21st century. 4. Terrorism--United States--Prevention. 5. Special operations (Military science)--United States. 6. Special operations (Military science)--Pakistan. 7. War on Terrorism, 2001-2009. I. Garbus, Julia.
    HV6430.B55A88 2015
    958.104'6092—dc23
    [B]
                                                                    2014021951

Printed in the United States of America
1 2 3 4 5 6 7 18 17 16 15 14

CONTENTS

A journalist recounts the dramatic events of the night of May 1–2, 2011, when US Navy SEALs raided Osama bin Laden's compound in Abbottabad, Pakistan.

CHAPTER 2   Controversies Surrounding the Assassination of Osama bin Laden

A former US attorney general argues that intelligence gathered using harsh interrogation techniques led to Bin Laden. He explains that the techniques are useful and legal.

John McCain

The senior senator from Arizona—a former prisoner of war—delivers an impassioned critique of the use of torture. He disputes the notion that so-called "harsh interrogation" techniques led to Osama bin Laden and argues that their use diminishes the United States and its war against terrorism.

Rupert Cornwell

A British journalist outlines the controversies regarding who actually killed Osama bin Laden. Summarizing the contradictory stories of the Navy SEALs who claim to have been the shooter, he concludes that the truth may never be known.

David Paul Kuhn

A journalist reports on the jubilation expressed by people around the United States after the announcement that Osama bin Laden had been killed. He writes that the assassination brought closure, particularly to 9/11 survivors and victims' families.

Harlan Ullman

An international policy and military adviser writes that the fight against al Qaeda and the hunt for Bin Laden has had many detrimental effects on the US economy, the national psyche, and its relations with other countries.

that the assassination of Osama bin Laden is meaningless, and the United States has made too many compromises in its "war on terror."

CHAPTER 3   Personal Narratives

raid on the Osama bin Laden compound and about the experience of watching the events in Abbottabad live from the White House's situation room.

A CNN producer reports on the thoughts of members of the national security team gathered in the White House's situation room the night of May 1–2, 2011.

FOREWORD

"History cannot give us a program for the future, but it can give us a fuller understanding of ourselves, and of our common humanity, so that we can better face the future."
—*Robert Penn Warren,*
American poet and novelist

The history of each nation is punctuated by momentous events that represent turning points for that nation, with an impact felt far beyond its borders. These events—displaying the full range of human capabilities, from violence, greed, and ignorance to heroism, courage, and strength—are nearly always complicated and multifaceted. Any student of history faces the challenge of grasping the many strands that constitute such world-changing events as wars, social movements, and environmental disasters. But understanding these significant historic events can be enhanced by exposure to a variety of perspectives, whether of people involved intimately or of ones observing from a distance of miles or years. Understanding can also be increased by learning about the controversies surrounding such events and exploring hot-button issues from multiple angles. Finally, true understanding of important historic events involves knowledge of the events' human impact—of the ways such events affected people in their everyday lives—all over the world.

Perspectives on Modern World History examines global historic events from the twentieth century onward by presenting analysis and observation from numerous vantage points. Each volume offers high school, early college level, and general interest readers a thematically arranged anthology of previously published materials that address a major historical event, with an emphasis on international coverage. Each volume opens with background information on the event, then presents the controversies surrounding that event, and concludes with first-person narratives from people who lived through the event or were affected by it. By providing primary sources from the time of the event, as well as relevant commentary surrounding the event, this series can be used to inform debate, help develop critical thinking skills, increase global awareness, and enhance an understanding of international perspectives on history.

Material in each volume is selected from a diverse range of sources, including journals, magazines, newspapers, nonfiction books, personal narratives, speeches, congressional testimony, government documents, pamphlets, organization newsletters, and position papers. Articles taken from these sources are carefully edited and introduced to provide context and background. Each volume of Perspectives on Modern World History includes an array of views on events of global significance. Much of the material comes from international sources and from US sources that provide extensive international coverage.

Each volume in the Perspectives on Modern World History series also includes:

- A full-color **world map**, offering context and geographic perspective.
- An annotated **table of contents** that provides a brief summary of each essay in the volume.
- An **introduction** specific to the volume topic.
- For each viewpoint, a brief **introduction** that has notes about the author and source of the viewpoint, and that provides a summary of its main points.
- Full-color **charts, graphs, maps**, and other visual representations.

- Informational **sidebars** that explore the lives of key individuals, give background on historical events, or explain scientific or technical concepts.
- A **glossary** that defines key terms, as needed.
- A **chronology** of important dates preceding, during, and immediately following the event.
- A **bibliography** of additional books, periodicals, and websites for further research.
- A comprehensive **subject index** that offers access to people, places, and events cited in the text.

Perspectives on Modern World History is designed for a broad spectrum of readers who want to learn more about not only history but also current events, political science, government, international relations, and sociology—students doing research for class assignments or debates, teachers and faculty seeking to supplement course materials, and others wanting to improve their understanding of history. Each volume of Perspectives on Modern World History is designed to illuminate a complicated event, to spark debate, and to show the human perspective behind the world's most significant happenings of recent decades.

INTRODUCTION

Most Americans had never heard of Osama bin Laden until September 20, 2001, when President George W. Bush addressed a nation stunned and frightened after the terrible events of 9/11. "The evidence we have gathered all points to a collection of loosely-affiliated terrorist organizations known as al-Qaeda," Bush said. "The group and its leader, Osama bin Laden, are linked to many other organizations in different countries."[1] And so Americans became familiar with a man whose army of radical Islamists had been wreaking destruction in other countries for more than thirteen years.

Before reading Bin Laden's story, it's important to understand that his beliefs are completely rejected by most Muslims, who overwhelmingly condemn violence, reject religious extremism, and view al Qaeda unfavorably. Islam's pillars are simple: declaring faith in God (Allah); praying; fasting; making a pilgrimage to Mohammed's birthplace, Mecca; and giving alms to the poor. However a small minority of Muslims fight to establish regimes based on strict religious law (sharia) and to eliminate non-Muslim influence from the Muslim world. They interpret the Muslim religious duty of jihad (struggle) not as an internal struggle against sin, as most Muslims do, but as a violent conflict against perceived enemies.

Born in Saudi Arabia in 1957, Bin Laden came from money. His father founded the largest construction company in the country, forging close ties with the Saudi royal family. At his father's death in 1969, the young Bin Laden reportedly inherited $80 million. Bin Laden's family members were devout Muslims but not extremists. In college Bin Laden became part of a fundamentalist

Muslim group. After college he moved to Afghanistan to join radical Islamic fighting forces (mujahideen) fighting the Soviet occupation. He used his inheritance to fund the fighters, run training camps, funnel weapons and fighters to the conflict, and build roads and shelters for the insurgents. Occasionally he took part in the fighting. In September 1988, Bin Laden and several other Islamic jihad leaders formed al Qaeda ("the base" in Arabic).

The Soviets withdrew from Afghanistan in 1989, and Bin Laden returned to Saudi Arabia as a jihad hero. The next year Saddam Hussein's Iraqi troops invaded Kuwait, putting Saudi Arabia and its royal family at risk of attack. Bin Laden suggested that the Saudi government use his mujahideens to defend the country. The government rejected his offer and instead invited in US troops, who drove the Iraqis from Kuwait in 1991. Outraged by the deployment of Americans near Muslim holy sites, Bin Laden heaped criticism on the Saudi government until they expelled him in 1991.

In 1992 Bin Laden settled in Sudan, where he sponsored training camps and solidified his plans to attack Americans. Al Qaeda's first attack on Americans was a hotel bombing in Yemen in 1992, which failed to kill the American targets. The next year, on October 3–4, 1993, Somali militia, probably trained by al Qaeda, shot down a US helicopter, leading to the "Black Hawk Down" battle in which eighteen Americans and many Somalis died. Bin Laden issued his first fatwa (religious proclamation) against the United States in 1996: "A Declaration of War Against the Americans Occupying the Land of Two Holy Places." Pressured by the United States and Saudi Arabia, Sudan expelled Bin Laden. He was allowed to choose a destination and returned to Afghanistan, welcomed by the Taliban, a radical Islamist group ruling the country. There he continued running training camps and bringing fighters, arms, and cash into Afghanistan.

Throughout the 1990s, al Qaeda's attacks intensified. The group massacred fifty-eight tourists in Luxor, Egypt, in 1997. In 1998 Bin Laden issued another fatwa stating that the US presence in Islamic holy lands is "a clear declaration of war" on Muslims, who have a duty to fight back. "The ruling to kill the Americans and their allies—civilian and military," Bin Laden declared, "is an individual duty for every Muslim who can do it in any country in which it is possible to do it."[2] The same year, on the eighth anniversary of US forces' entrance into Saudi Arabia, al Qaeda engineered simultaneous truck bomb explosions at two US embassies in East Africa, killing 240 people. The United States began trying to capture or kill Bin Laden after the embassy bombings, getting close as many as ten times. The nation planned a cruise missile attack on an al Qaeda training camp; trained Pakistanis to hunt Bin Laden; and attacked a convoy of vehicles in the Afghan mountains . . . all to no avail.

Bin Laden planned an even more ambitious attack to mark the millennium: On January 1–3, 2000, bombs would explode at tourist sites in Jordan, at Los Angeles International Airport (LAX), and on a US Navy ship, *The Sullivans*. Luckily officials discovered the Jordan and LAX attacks before they could occur, and the small boat headed for the US ship sank before detonating. But in October 2000, a similar attack on a US ship succeeded, killing seventeen soldiers on the USS *Cole* in Yemen.

The most extensive attempt to capture Bin Laden occurred in late 2001 at Tora Bora, a cave complex in Afghanistan where Bin Laden and his followers had holed up. Over the course of several weeks, American and British soldiers dropped 700,000 pounds of bombs on the area and battled al Qaeda forces. When allied forces finally overcame al Qaeda and searched the cave complex, Bin Laden was gone.

Meanwhile the United States embarked on a "war on terror" as a response to 9/11. When the Taliban refused to hand over Bin Laden after 9/11, the United States invaded Afghanistan. The Taliban fell but fighting continued, claiming more than three thousand US coalition lives. (The United States plans to completely withdraw from the Afghan conflict by the end of 2014.) In 2003 the US invaded Iraq, although al Qaeda had little presence there. President Bush told the nation, "Iraq is now the central front of the war on terror. Enemies of freedom are making a desperate stand there."[3] Troops quickly deposed dictator Saddam Hussein—but about 4,500 soldiers died during the United States' eight years in Iraq.

While soldiers fought, intelligence officers spent the first decade of the millennium struggling to track down the elusive al Qaeda mastermind. Most people thought Bin Laden was in Pakistan, but no one knew where. Interrogators tried to wrest information from Taliban and al Qaeda prisoners in secret facilities abroad or at Guantanamo Bay, a detention camp on a US naval base in Cuba. These interrogators used coercive techniques that some have described as torture. For example, waterboarding involves pouring water over an immobilized captive to simulate the sensation of drowning; Khalid Sheikh Mohammed, the planner of 9/11, was waterboarded 183 times. Less harsh interrogation techniques were used as well, and it's disputed whether coercive techniques in particular led to information about Bin Laden's whereabouts. Guantanamo detainees eventually pointed interrogators to a courier who funneled information and supplies to Bin Laden. The CIA learned the courier's name by 2007. Painstaking stakeouts, surveillance, and interceptions of communications followed.

In August 2010, a Pakistani CIA employee followed the courier's Suzuki jeep to a fortress-like compound in Abbottabad, Pakistan, a suburb of the country's capital. The CIA rented a house in the town and monitored the compound intensively. Surrounded by concrete walls topped with barbed wire, complete with security gates and privacy walls, the space seemed custom-built to hide an important person. One of its residents, a tall, thin man who frequently walked around a vegetable garden, was dubbed "the Pacer" by analysts. Analysts suspected he was Bin Laden, but could not get a good picture of the man's face. Some analysts put the probability that it was Bin Laden at 60 percent, others at 80 percent. The percentages were high enough to begin planning an attack.

Three options were considered: dropping a small bomb directly on the compound, using a drone to fire a small missile at "the Pacer," or sending in the SEALs (Sea, Air and Land teams), the Navy's elite special operations force. The bomb idea was abandoned; any bomb powerful enough to destroy a suspected underground bunker would kill everyone in the compound and destroy houses outside it. A small missile might miss "the Pacer," who would then flee. After a restless night pondering the options, President Barack Obama chose the raid.

Perspectives on Modern World History: The Assassination of Osama bin Laden delves into the controversies surrounding the extensive—and expensive—manhunt for Bin Laden. Was the war on terror an appropriate response to al Qaeda? Are coercive interrogation techniques effective? What exactly happened during the SEALs' mission? Has Bin Laden's death made the world safer? Three years after the raid on Abbottabad in 2011, the debates continue.

Notes

1. "Text: President Bush Addresses the Nation," *Washington Post*, September 20, 2011. www.washingtonpost.com.
2. "Jihad Against Jews and Crusaders," World Islamic Front Statement, February 23, 1998. www.fas.org.
3. George W. Bush, "A Central Front in the War on Terror," September 9, 2003. http://georgewbush-whitehouse.archives.gov.

World Map

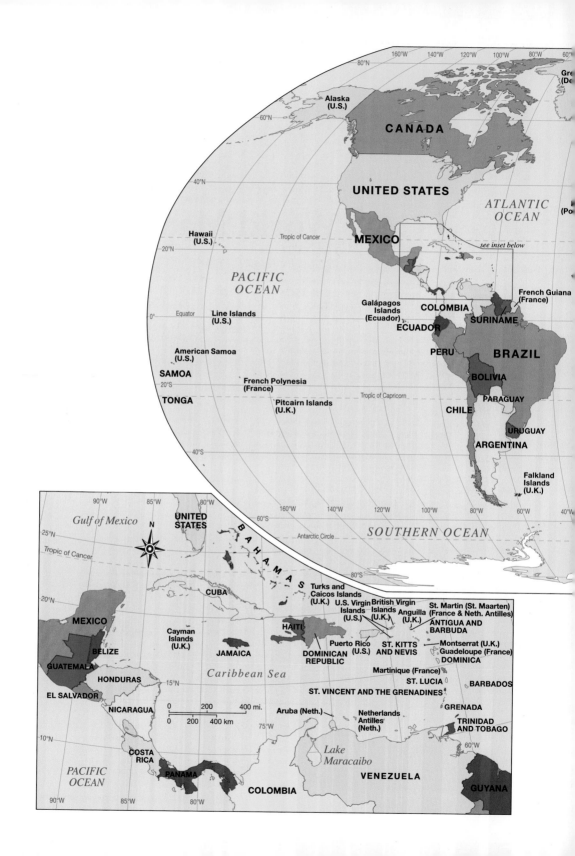

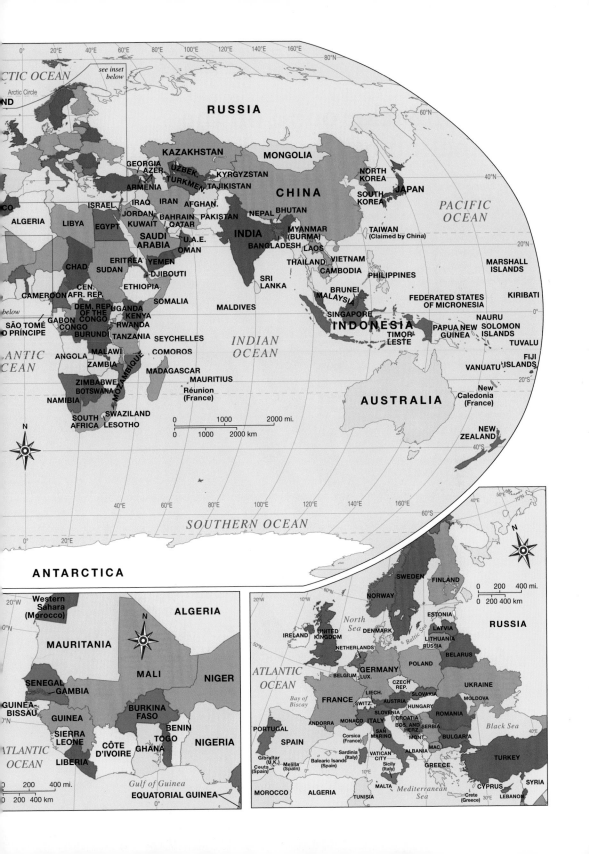

CHAPTER 1

Historical Background on the Assassination of Osama bin Laden

Al Qaeda: Osama bin Laden's Terrorist Organization

Mathieu Guidère

In the following viewpoint, a historical encyclopedia of religion explains the history of al Qaeda, the terrorist organization founded by Osama bin Laden in 1988. The viewpoint explains the organization's ideology, which is based on the belief that a holy war, or jihad, will lead to a pan-Islamist state. Their beliefs are also based on the Islamic Revival, a movement that dates to the 1970s. The author explains that al Qaeda's development and rise are divided into four primary sections, beginning in the period of the Soviet-Afghan War. By the early twenty-first century, the organization spread not only throughout most of the Middle East, but also through parts of Africa and even in the United States. The viewpoint describes how US interventions in Iraq and Afghanistan after the September 11, 2001, attacks helped al Qaeda increase its influence in some areas and how

Photo on opposite page: Crowds gather near the World Trade Center site in New York the night of May 2, 2011, to celebrate the news that Osama bin Laden is dead. (© Jason DeCrow/ AP Images.)

SOURCE. Mathieu Guidère, "Al Qaeda: Osama bin Laden's Terrorist Organization," *Historical Dictionary of Islamic Fundamentalism.* New York: Scarecrow Press, 2012. Copyright © 2012 by Rowman & Littlefield. All rights reserved. Reproduced by permission.

Bin Laden's assassination affected the organization's leadership and morale. Mathieu Guidère, a professor at the University of Toulouse II-Le Mirail, is the author of a number of books on Islam and the Arab world. His research has focused on the psychology of terrorism and radicalism as well as ideological trends in Islamist movements.

This global, multifaceted Sunni Islamic fundamentalist umbrella group is probably the most well-known extremist and terrorist organization in the world. Founded by the Saudi Osama bin Laden in August 1988, al-Qaeda's ideological platform hinges on the necessity of the jihad to establish a pan-Islamic state. Al-Qaeda has claimed responsibility for numerous attacks and the deaths of thousands over the past two decades. Its World Trade Center and Pentagon attacks of September 11, 2001 even prompted the U.S. "War on Terror" campaign, which began in October 2001 and continued officially until President Barack Obama declared an "end" to his predecessor's "war on terror" on 23 January 2009. However, it was the East African United States Embassy attacks in 1998 that originally brought al-Qaeda to the attention of the media.

Ideologically, the group is totally against any Western presence or non-Muslim influences, seeks the establishment of a caliphate and the implementation of *sharia* (Islamic law), and even opposes schools of Islam that are not Sunni (leading to even more sectarian violence). In 1998, al-Qaeda was also known under the name "International Islamic Front for Jihad against the Crusaders and the Jews"—further illustrating its agenda. The term "al-Qaeda," interestingly enough, comes from the Arabic word meaning "base." This refers to fundamentals as a base and a militaristic type of base. Although the group dominates the contemporary jihadist movement and influences many other groups, it is by no means the only driving force behind contemporary Islamic fundamentalist extremism.

Group Organization and Tactics

> *Al-Qaeda has several thousand adherents and has even aligned itself with other like-minded militant groups.*

After Osama bin Laden's death on 2 May 2011, Ayman al-Zawahiri was made *amir* [leader] of the organization on 16 June 2011. The *shura* [consultation] council of al-Qaeda consists of an estimated 20 to 30 people who transmit orders among the various al-Qaeda groups and still remains a unified but decentralized whole. Under the shura council, there is also a military committee that focuses its efforts on recruitment, training, arms acquisition, and tactical intelligence. A committee that concerns itself only with monetary funding of the group also exists. Through the *hawala* [a Middle Eastern financial network that operates outside traditional banking methods] system, members of this committee ensure the financial solvency of al-Qaeda. There are also committees that deal with issuing *fatwas* [decrees], reviewing Islamic law decrees, and providing media outlets (in 2005, the As-Sahab production team was created in order to maintain all media communication facilities internally).

With regard to membership, al-Qaeda has several thousand adherents and has even aligned itself with other like-minded militant groups—in some cases absorbing them into the al-Qaeda organization and creating new branches (as is the case with al-Qaeda in Iraq and al-Qaeda in the Islamic Maghreb). It is also common practice for groups to pledge (*bay'a*) their alliance not only to al-Qaeda but also to its leaders when creating relationships. In doing this, it is perceived that all actions that the newly aligned group undertakes are therefore in the name of al-Qaeda as a whole. In addition, the group's leadership is highly decentralized and therefore efficient in both delegation and execution.

> "The use of suicide bombings . . . has projected the issue of Islamic martyrdom into Western knowledge."

Since al-Qaeda is present in multiple countries and continents, this type of structure is the key to its internal stability. The groups that directly fall under the banner of al-Qaeda include the East Turkestan Islamic Movement, the Egyptian Islamic Jihad, the Somali Shebaab Movement (Harakat al-Shabaab), the Libyan Islamic Fighting Group, al-Qaeda in the Arabian Peninsula, al-Qaeda in Iraq, and al-Qaeda in the Islamic Maghreb.

Strategic and Ideological Basis

Tactically, the group implements primarily the use of suicide bombings and could be considered the group that has projected the issue of Islamic martyrdom into Western knowledge. Al-Qaeda has even issued fatwas to justify its jihad. It has been estimated that the militants active in the al-Qaeda system are so well trained, well organized, and numerous that they could easily carry out the missions of the father group without ever being given any direct orders. They could also sustain themselves quite well if ever communications were completely cut off from al-Qaeda leaders and its cadres. This military effectiveness is due partly to the fact that many members of the al-Qaeda forces are Afghan Arabs and former *mujahideen* [guerrilla fighters] and therefore are in possession of vast experience and tactical knowledge. Al-Qaeda has also taken advantage of domestic terrorist tactics as well as international ones. The domestic tactics are unique in that they target the people of their country and its leaders in the hope of toppling the regime and undermining the economy, which would then destroy the state and make way for the desired Islamic state to be established.

It can be argued that the ideology of al-Qaeda has its basis in the Islamic revivalist movement, which has been

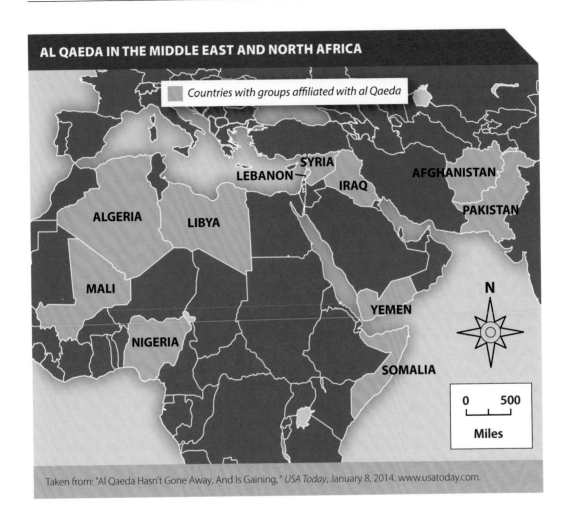

AL QAEDA IN THE MIDDLE EAST AND NORTH AFRICA

Countries with groups affiliated with al Qaeda

SYRIA
LEBANON
IRAQ
AFGHANISTAN
PAKISTAN
ALGERIA
LIBYA
MALI
YEMEN
NIGERIA
SOMALIA

N

0   500
Miles

Taken from: "Al Qaeda Hasn't Gone Away, And Is Gaining," *USA Today*, January 8, 2014. www.usatoday.com.

operating throughout the Muslim world for the past half century. Sayyid Qutb has also been noted as being the most influential radical Islamic thinker who has influenced the group. The organization has developed this austere notion of Islam into not only an ideology but also a way of life. Following Qutb's discourses, to al-Qaeda adherents, Islamic fundamentalism should dictate all facets of everyday life for the devoted Muslim—going beyond mere worship. The present leader of al-Qaeda, al-Zawahiri (who also was second in command to bin Laden), strongly supported Qutb's ideologies and studied them at length. Probably the most influential of Qutb's discourses was the idea that apostates could be prosecuted under sharia, which would therefore give legitimacy to al-Qaeda's jihad.

Historical Development

The formation and rise of al-Qaeda can be divided into four sections: development, consolidation, growth, and networking. The development period started with the Soviet-Afghan War (1979–1989). As the communist forces began to take control of Afghanistan, the United States became involved in order to thwart the advances of the Eastern bloc troops. As the Afghan Arabs launched their jihad against the Soviet Union, the United States began to provide them with tactical and military support, fueling their fight. Many of these mujahideen were also adherents of the extremist brand of Islam, so, in providing for the mujahideen, the United States was also promoting the Islamic radicals by proxy. During this time, Osama bin Laden was also rising in the Afghan Arab ranks and by the close of the insurgency was one of its leading fighters. Meanwhile, prominent Islamists also began to notice the vigor that the mujahideen displayed during the war, especially after finally expelling the Soviet troops in 1989. Many affluent Muslims (especially from Saudi Arabia) started donating money to the mujahideen cause and created camps for them within Afghanistan. However, this resulted in many of the Afghan Arabs being displaced, and various alliances were formed in an almost chaotic manner.

While these various groups of fighters were living austerely, there seemed to be a common belief that their Islamic program should not be restricted only to Afghanistan. Many wanted to continue their jihad in other areas. Of these many pockets of fighters, one was led by bin Laden. This group held its first meetings in August 1988. While still in Afghanistan, the group constructed

its platform of Islamic fundamentalism and proclaimed its further promotion of the jihad. Soon, other similar groups joined bin Laden's plea that unity among the Islamists would lead to greater advances.

After leaving Afghanistan in 1990, bin Laden returned to his native Saudi Arabia and offered the kingdom the assistance of his militant force—an assistance that was needed because of the Iraqi invasion of Kuwait in August of that year that threatened Saudi Arabia. When al-Saud turned down the help of al-Qaeda forces in favor of American military aid, the group went to Sudan in 1992. Here, the pan-Islamic ideas began to spread, especially in light of Saudi Arabia seeking non-Muslim help for the protection of the lands that are integral to Islam (Mecca and Medina). Al-Qaeda was welcomed in Sudan by Hassan al-Turabi, and time that members spent there was interesting, especially since the

Osama bin Laden addresses his supporters in a video leaked to the media in October 2001. Al Qaeda has employed a number of media—including video and sound recordings and, more recently, social networking—to communicate with and galvanize its members. (© Gamma-Rapho via Getty Images.)

country had just experienced a military coup d'état that resulted in the government being revamped on the basis of Islamic ideals. This made it even easier for al-Qaeda to spread and grow.

Meanwhile, the Egyptian Islamic Jihad (which was now an intrinsic segment of al-Qaeda) was becoming more aggressive in its attacks in Egypt, and bin Laden's verbal criticism against Saudi Arabia was increasing as well. These events eventually resulted in the al-Qaeda organization being exiled from Sudan in 1996 because of international pressure on the Sudanese government. The group then returned to Afghanistan and rejoined its mujahideen brothers who had remained in the country. This was the same year that the Taliban army rose to power in Afghanistan. Ideologically and structurally similar to al-Qaeda, the group already had strong support from the Afghan Arabs, and al-Qaeda soon came to recognize its legitimacy. In September 1996, the Taliban captured the capital of Kabul and claimed the land as the "Islamic Amirate of Afghanistan." This atmosphere in Afghanistan made it possible for al-Qaeda to develop and propagate itself freely. The two groups began to rule the country with a shared militancy and were largely insulated from any opposing forces. Although the Taliban army was declared the official rulers of the land, they provided al-Qaeda with a cover of protection.

> Al-Qaeda [has] effectively spread its pan-Islamic jihadist program through most of the Middle East, North Africa, and parts of Asia.

In Kashmir, al-Qaeda also attracted the interest of the Harakat-ul-Mujahideen organization, which declared its support of the former's jihad against the West in 1998. The group was attracted to al-Qaeda's rage against the West (and specifically the American forces) since the West's diplomatic relations with India supported the Indian acquisition of the Jammu and Kashmir regions. This support clearly caused separatist groups such as Harakat-ul-Mujahideen to favor any military front that would be conducive to the removal of Jammu and Kashmir from Indian control. Al-Qaeda's supposed relationship with Pakistan's Inter-Services Intelligence also further supported this alignment. In 2001, there were also reports that Harakat-ul-Mujahideen was harboring bin Laden and other high-profile al-Qaeda leaders within the Pakistani-controlled portions of Kashmir. Pakistani-based Kashmiri groups such as Harakat-ul-Jihad al-Islami, Jaish-e-Muhammad, and Lashkar-e-Tayyiba have also been allegedly affiliated with al-Qaeda. These allegations are due to the relationship that many leaders within these groups have with al-Qaeda senior officers.

Effects of 9/11 and Subsequent U.S. Interventions

However, after the 11 September 2001 World Trade Center and Pentagon attacks when U.S. forces entered Afghanistan, the Taliban army (which refused to surrender bin Laden) was swiftly ousted, and al-Qaeda relocated to the Pakistani border. Yet, by this time, despite the American pressure, al-Qaeda had already effectively spread its pan-Islamic jihadist program through most of the Middle East, North Africa, and parts of Asia through its vast system of networking.

The American presence in the Middle East did result in some advantages for al-Qaeda, however. For example, when U.S. forces toppled the Baathist Iraqi regime in 2003, this allowed many Islamic groups (which were formerly repressed) to grow within the country. Al-Qaeda saw this as a beneficial event and in September 2004 established al-Qaeda in Iraq after aligning itself with Abu Musab al-Zarqawi's Jamaat al-Tawhid wa al-Jihad. Within Iraq, the Shiite community (which was arguably the most repressed group during the Baathist regime) began to increase its influence, and the Sunni al-Qaeda saw this union as a chance to undercut these efforts. A jihad against Iraqi Shiites was then declared, and many Shiite people and locations were attacked by Tanzim Qaidat al-Jihad fi Bilad al-Rafidayn (Organization of Jihad's Base in the Land of Two Rivers; al-Qaeda in Iraq's official title). This sectarian violence, marked mostly by suicide bombings, came to a peak by 2007.

By the middle of the decade, al-Qaeda also began to concentrate a majority of its training camps and bases along the Afghanistan-Pakistan border and gain influence in African nations like Algeria, Mali, and Somalia. On 11 September 2006, al-Qaeda in the Islamic Maghreb was officially announced and has been active in the Sahara Desert regions of the continent. Since its inception, the group has grown into a formidable force, and violence in North Africa has increased because of it. It became such an influential force in the African country that, by 2009, Somalia's al-Shabaab pledged allegiance to al-Qaeda. Because of bin Laden's animosity against the Saudi regime, an al-Qaeda network was placed there for quite some time and in January 2009 merged itself with its comrades in Yemen to form al-Qaeda in the Arabian Peninsula and based itself in Yemen.

Spreading al-Qaeda's Ideology Worldwide

Even in the United States, al-Qaeda has contingents. The most notorious leader was Anwar al-Awlaki. A spiritual motivator and Islamic recruiter, almost every notable al-Qaeda affiliate that has been on American soil has had a relationship with him. These include three of the 11 September 2001 hijackers, Fort Hood shooter Nidal Malik Hasan, and possibly John Phillip Walker Lindh. For the past decade, he was the primary American-born voice in promotion of the jihad against the Western forces. Al-Awlaki was successful in using propaganda methods, such as his online publication *Inspire*, which effectively combines Western communication techniques and Islamic ideological content.

> " The Internet has proven to be a viable and fluid tool for the organization to spread its ideologies. "

With regard to communication of propaganda, since 2001, al-Qaeda has focused almost all its efforts on online media outlets. Since publication of periodicals or pamphlets and the like is too easily restricted in many of the countries in which the group located, the Internet has proven to be a viable and fluid tool for the organization to spread its ideologies. Over the years, its methods have increased in both sophistication and breadth. Its forums now encompass a variety of subjects and can be accessed in multiple languages in various countries. The publicity that the Internet has provided for the group has become an invaluable resource for its networking, financing, and recruitment as well. A variety of media is also used, such as videos, sound recordings, photographs, and testimonials. Many are impressively stylized and use common master narratives that are easily recognizable and relatable to the group's audience. In addition, by creating its own online platforms, al-Qaeda avoids the risk of other third-party distributors editing or removing significant portions of its content. However, many of these sites and online publications are highly monitored and often are swiftly removed by internal security agents in a large number of countries.

Although the al-Qaeda network has continued to spread its ideologies and remains the most formidable jihadist organization in the world, the group is by no means supported by a large number of Islamic fundamentalists. The group's brutality against fellow Muslims and its civilian domestic violence have been the main causes of opposition by many Islamic scholars and militants. Many moderate Islamists also do not fully support the jihadi doctrine against the West or are highly critical of it and therefore of al-Qaeda since it is al-Qaeda's primary ideology. Interestingly enough, one of the first supporters of al-Qaeda, Egyptian Islamic Jihad ideologue Sayyed Imam al-Sharif, even retracted his support for the group in his 2007 publication *Wathiqat Tarshid Al-'Amal Al-Jihadi fi Misr wa al-'Alam* (Rationalizing Jihad in Egypt and the World). The general public's support of al-Qaeda in many countries has also been slowly declining since 2008, according to reports. Yet the organization continues to prosper throughout Africa, the Middle East, and South Asia.

Although there is no doubt that the 2 May 2011 death of bin Laden had an impact on al-Qaeda's morale, the group proved resilient and has been persistent in its insistence that although the group owed a big debt to him and that he was an obvious asset, he was merely one man. Al-Qaeda continued by stating that the movement is greater than one person but that bin Laden will always be held up as one of the greatest martyrs because of his accomplishments. Throughout the 2011 events of the Arab Spring, al-Qaeda initially remained rather quiet despite many reports that certain demonstrations were instigated by the organization. As the year passed, al-Qaeda eventually announced more and more support for various rebellions, but it seems as if the group is letting the events fully take their course before influencing the newly rearranged states.

Terror Memos Authorized Harsh Interrogation Techniques

Warren Richey

The following viewpoint describes the immediate aftermath of the 2009 release of US government memos authorizing harsh interrogation techniques for terrorism-related detainees. Human rights experts classify the techniques as torture, the viewpoint explains, but in the memos the government argues that the techniques do not qualify as such. The viewpoint reports that the memos were released due to actions by the American Civil Liberties Union, which considers the US government's actions as tantamount to war crimes. The interrogation policies detailed in the memos were created by the administration of US president George W. Bush. Although the administration of Barack Obama discontinued the practices, it also declined to prosecute those who used the techniques. Warren Richey has been a staff writer for the *Christian Science Monitor* for more than twenty years and worked previously as a journalist in the Middle East writing for the *Saudi Gazette*, among other publications.

The Obama administration will not prosecute US intelligence officials involved in harsh interrogations of terror suspects, the president pledged on Thursday.

The assurance came as the Justice Department released four secret memos used during the Bush presidency offering legal justification for interrogation techniques that human rights experts classify as torture, such as waterboarding.

The action comes after weeks of heated debate within the administration over whether to release the memos. Some officials were concerned that public disclosure might help Al Qaeda and build momentum for investigation of alleged acts of torture by US intelligence officials.

> Within days of taking office, Mr. Obama ended the use of harsh interrogation techniques described in the memos.

Many human rights activists have urged the president to authorize an investigation of torture allegations during President Bush's war on terror, with some calling for the appointment of an independent prosecutor.

But the president and Attorney General Eric Holder have decided against that. "This is a time for reflection, not retribution," President Obama said in a statement released by the White House. "We have been through a dark and painful chapter in our history. But at a time of great challenges and disturbing disunity, nothing will be gained by spending our time and energy laying blame for the past."

Human rights activists blasted the decision.

Within days of taking office, Mr. Obama ended the use of harsh interrogation techniques described in the memos.

One memo, dated August 2002, authorized 10 special interrogation techniques for use against Al Qaeda suspect Abu Zubaydah, including waterboarding. Under this interrogation technique, the suspect is placed on a board or table with his feet above his head, a cloth is draped over the nose and mouth, and water is poured over his face.

The technique, widely considered a form of torture by human-rights experts, triggers an intense, uncontrollable sensation of drowning.

In the memo, then Assistant Attorney General Jay Bybee acknowledged that waterboarding came close to violating the US torture statute because it constitutes "a threat of imminent death." But he added that it would not amount to torture unless the experience resulted in "prolonged mental harm" lasting months or years.

"In the absence of prolonged mental harm, no severe mental pain or suffering would have been inflicted, and the use of these procedures would not constitute torture within the meaning of the statute," Mr. Bybee wrote.

> 'Officials at the highest level of government authorized and gave legal blessing to acts of torture that violate domestic and international law.'

Questions had been raised about Mr. Abu Zubaydah's mental health, based in part on his actions in court proceedings at Guantanamo.

The memos were pried out of government secrecy as a result of a Freedom of Information Act lawsuit filed by the American Civil Liberties Union (ACLU). Had the administration not released the memos voluntarily, a judge would probably have ordered it to do so, analysts say.

ACLU lawyers said they were pleased the documents were released, but criticized the president's decision not to prosecute. "Enforcing the nation's laws should not be a political decision," said ACLU executive director Anthony Romero. "These memos provide yet more

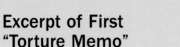

Excerpt of First "Torture Memo"

August 1, 2002

Memorandum for Alberto R. Gonzales, Counsel to the President

Re: Standards of Conduct for Interrogation Under 18 U.S.C. §§ 2340-2340A

You have asked for our Office's views regarding the standards of conduct under the Convention Against Torture and Other Cruel, Inhuman and Degrading Treatment or Punishment as implemented by Sections 2340-2340A of title 18 of the United States Code. As we understand it, this question has arisen in the context of the conduct of interrogations outside of the United States. . . .

We conclude that torture as defined in and proscribed by Sections 2340-2340A, covers only extreme acts. Severe pain is generally of the kind difficult for the victim to endure. Where the pain is physical, it must be of an intensity akin to that which accompanies serious physical injury such as death or organ failure. Severe mental pain requires suffering not just at the moment of infliction but it also requires lasting psychological harm, such as seen in mental disorders like posttraumatic stress disorder. Additionally, such severe mental pain can arise only from the predicate acts listed in Section 2340. Because the acts inflicting torture are extreme, there is significant range of acts that though they might constitute cruel, inhuman, or degrading treatment or punishment fail to rise to the level of torture.

Further, we conclude that under the circumstances of the current war against al Qaeda and its allies, application of Section 2340A to interrogations undertaken pursuant to the President's Commander-in-Chief powers may be unconstitutional. Finally, even if an interrogation method might violate Section 2340A, necessity or self-defense could provide justifications that would eliminate any criminal liability.

Please let us know if we can be of further assistance.

Jay S. Bybee

Jay S. Bybee
Assistant Attorney General

SOURCE. *"Memorandum for Alberto Gonzales, Counsel to the President, Re: Standards of Conduct for Interrogation Under 18 U.S.C. §§ 2340-2340A,"* The Torture Memos: Rationalizing the Unthinkable, *David Cole, ed. New York: The New Press, 2009, pp. 41, 99–100.*

incontrovertible evidence that Bush administration officials at the highest level of government authorized and gave legal blessing to acts of torture that violate domestic and international law," he says.

In addition to waterboarding, the 2002 Bybee memo authorized slapping, pushing, confinement in a small, dark space, painful stress positions, and sleep deprivation for up to 11 days. It also approved a request to lock Abu Zubaydah in a confinement box with an insect.

The memo says: "You have informed us that he appears to have a fear of insects. In particular, you would like to tell Abu Zubaydah that you intend to place a stinging insect into the box with him."

Bybee says the plan would be to trick Abu Zubaydah into thinking he was about to be stung. "You have orally informed us that you would in fact place a harmless insect, such as a caterpillar, in the box with him," Bybee wrote.

"Through these memos, Justice Department lawyers authorized interrogators to use the most barbaric interrogation methods, including methods that the US once prosecuted as war crimes," Jameel Jaffer, director of the ACLU's National Security Project, said in a statement.

The president and attorney general emphasized that US officials who acted reasonably and relied on the legal advice in the memos would not be charged and face a criminal trial for torture.

Attorney General Holder said he'd informed the CIA that the government would provide legal representation, at no cost to government officials, in any legal proceeding concerning illegal interrogation methods. The pledge extends to international and foreign tribunals, Holder said.

> 'It would be unfair to prosecute dedicated men and women working to protect America for conduct that was sanctioned in advance by the Justice Department.'

Al Qaeda and Taliban detainees are watched by guards in an outside area of the Guantanamo Bay detention center in early 2002. Later that year, the US government authorized the use of enhanced interrogation techniques on enemy combatants such as these men. (© Shane T. McCoy/US Navy/AP Images.)

The government would also indemnify any employee for any money damages ordered paid to torture or abuse victims and would provide representation in any congressional investigation.

"It would be unfair to prosecute dedicated men and women working to protect America for conduct that was sanctioned in advance by the Justice Department," Holder said.

Amnesty International executive director Larry Cox criticized the administration's decision not to prosecute. "The Department of Justice appears to be offering a get-out-of-jail-free card to individuals who, by US Attorney General Eric Holder's own estimation, were involved in acts of torture," Mr. Cox said in a statement.

SEALs Assassinate Bin Laden in Pakistan

Nicholas Schmidle

The following viewpoint recounts the dramatic events of May 1 and May 2, 2011, culminating in Osama bin Laden's death in a Pakistan suburb. The author uses the accounts of US Navy SEALs (Sea, Air and Land teams) and officials briefed on the proceedings to tell the step-by-step story from the point of view of the personnel directly involved in the raid. The operation involved two stealth Black Hawk helicopters and four Chinook helicopters deployed as backup. Upon arriving at the Bin Laden compound, the first helicopter ran into trouble, and the pilot maneuvered a controlled crash landing in the yard, as animals scattered about. The soldiers made their way through a number of walls and areas of the compound before they reached the inner areas of the main house, blasting through locks and walls and killing a number of people on the way. Once they reached the private bedrooms, they finally found Osama bin Laden, who was initially shielded by a number of his wives, and killed him. The commotion brought out curious neighbors, including women and young children—none knew or admitted that they knew their neighbor was Bin Laden. Nicholas Schmidle is a staff writer at the *New Yorker* and a fellow at the New America Foundation. His writing has also appeared in the *New York Times Magazine*, *The Atlantic*, the *New Republic*, and *Slate*.

Shortly after eleven o'clock on the night of May 1st [2011], two MH-60 Black Hawk helicopters lifted off from Jalalabad Air Field, in eastern Afghanistan, and embarked on a covert mission into Pakistan to kill Osama bin Laden. Inside the aircraft were twenty-three Navy SEALs from Team Six, which is officially known as the Naval Special Warfare Development Group, or DEVGRU. A Pakistani-American translator, whom I will call Ahmed, and a dog named Cairo—a Belgian Malinois—were also aboard. It was a moonless evening, and the helicopters' pilots, wearing night-vision goggles, flew without lights over mountains that straddle the border with Pakistan. Radio communications were kept to a minimum, and an eerie calm settled inside the aircraft. . . .

> "Bin Laden was holed up on the third floor of a house in a one-acre compound [in a] middle-class neighborhood."

The Black Hawks, each of which had two pilots and a crewman from the 160th Special Operations Aviation Regiment, or the Night Stalkers, had been modified to mask heat, noise, and movement; the copters' exteriors had sharp, flat angles and were covered with radar-dampening "skin."

The SEALs' destination was a house in the small city of Abbottabad, which is about a hundred and twenty miles across the Pakistan border. Situated north of Islamabad, Pakistan's capital, Abbottabad is in the foothills of the Pir Panjal Range, and is popular in the summertime with families seeking relief from the blistering heat farther south. Founded in 1853 by a British major named James Abbott, the city became the home of a prestigious military academy after the creation of Pakistan, in 1947. According to information gathered by the Central Intelligence Agency, bin Laden was holed up on the third floor of a house in a one-acre compound just off Kakul Road in Bilal Town, a middle-class neighborhood less than a mile from the entrance to the academy. If all went according to plan, the SEALs would drop from the helicopters into the compound, overpower bin Laden's guards, shoot and kill him at close range, and then take the corpse back to Afghanistan. . . .

Black Hawks and Chinooks Depart for Abbottabad

Forty-five minutes after the Black Hawks departed, four MH-47 Chinooks launched from the same runway in Jalalabad. Two of them flew to the border, staying on the Afghan side; the other two proceeded into Pakistan. Deploying four Chinooks was a last-minute decision made after President Barack Obama said he wanted to feel assured that the Americans could "fight their way out of Pakistan." Twenty-five additional SEALs from DEVGRU, pulled from a squadron stationed in Afghanistan, sat in the Chinooks that remained at the border; this "quick-reaction force" would be called into action only if the mission went seriously wrong. The third and fourth Chinooks were each outfitted with a pair of M134 Miniguns. They followed the Black Hawks' initial flight path but landed at a predetermined point on a dry riverbed in a wide, unpopulated valley in northwest Pakistan. The nearest house was half a mile away. On the ground, the copters' rotors were kept whirring while operatives monitored the surrounding hills for encroaching Pakistani helicopters or fighter jets. One of the Chinooks was carrying fuel bladders, in case the other aircraft needed to refill their tanks.

Meanwhile, the two Black Hawks were quickly approaching Abbottabad from the northwest, hiding behind the mountains on the northernmost edge of the city. Then the pilots banked right and went south along a ridge that marks Abbottabad's eastern perimeter. When those hills tapered off, the pilots curled right again, toward the city center, and made their final approach.

During the next four minutes, the interior of the Black Hawks rustled alive with the metallic cough of rounds being chambered. Mark, a master chief petty officer and the ranking noncommissioned officer on the operation, crouched on one knee beside the open door of the lead helicopter. He and the eleven other SEALs on "helo one," who were wearing gloves and had on night-vision goggles, were preparing to fast-rope into bin Laden's yard. They waited for the crew chief to give the signal to throw the rope. But, as the pilot passed over the compound, pulled into a high hover, and began lowering

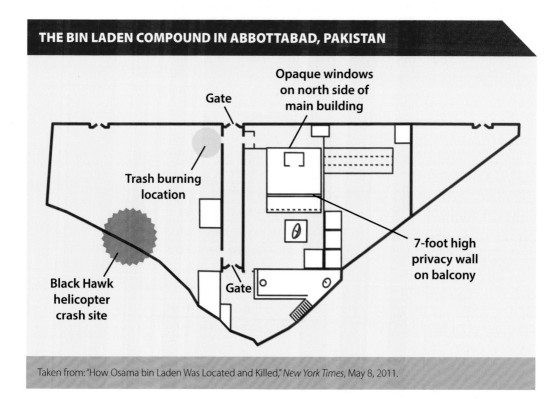

THE BIN LADEN COMPOUND IN ABBOTTABAD, PAKISTAN

Gate

Opaque windows on north side of main building

Trash burning location

7-foot high privacy wall on balcony

Black Hawk helicopter crash site

Gate

Taken from: "How Osama bin Laden Was Located and Killed," *New York Times*, May 8, 2011.

the aircraft, he felt the Black Hawk getting away from him. He sensed that they were going to crash. . . .

Tense Moments While Landing at the Compound

When the helicopter began getting away from the pilot, he pulled back on the cyclic, which controls the pitch of the rotor blades, only to find the aircraft unresponsive. The high walls of the compound and the warm temperatures had caused the Black Hawk to descend inside its own rotor wash—a hazardous aerodynamic situation known as "settling with power." . . . A former helicopter pilot with extensive special-operations experience said of the pilot's situation, "It's pretty spooky—I've been in it myself. The only way to get out of it is to push the cyclic forward and fly out of this vertical silo you're dropping through. That solution requires altitude. If you're settling with power at two thousand feet, you've got plenty of time to recover. If you're settling with power at fifty feet, you're going to hit the ground."

The pilot scrapped the plan to fast-rope and focused on getting the aircraft down. He aimed for an animal pen in the western section of the compound. The SEALs on board braced themselves as the tail rotor swung around, scraping the security wall. The pilot jammed the nose forward to drive it into the dirt and prevent his aircraft from rolling onto its side. Cows, chickens, and rabbits scurried. With the Black Hawk pitched at a forty-five-degree angle astride the wall, the crew sent a distress call to the idling Chinooks.

[Squadron commander] James and the SEALs in helo two watched all this while hovering over the compound's northeast corner. The second pilot, unsure whether his colleagues were taking fire or experiencing mechanical problems, ditched his plan

> The teams had barely been on target for a minute, and the mission was already veering off course.

to hover over the roof. Instead, he landed in a grassy field across the street from the house.

No American was yet inside the residential part of the compound. Mark and his team were inside a downed helicopter at one corner, while James and his team were at the opposite end. The teams had barely been on target for a minute, and the mission was already veering off course. . . .

After a few minutes, the twelve SEALs inside helo one recovered their bearings and calmly relayed on the radio that they were proceeding with the raid. . . .

Inside the Walls of bin Laden's Compound

Minutes after hitting the ground, Mark and the other team members began streaming out the side doors of helo one. Mud sucked at their boots as they ran alongside a ten-foot-high wall that enclosed the animal pen. A three-man demolition unit hustled ahead to the pen's closed metal gate, reached into bags containing explosives, and placed C-4 charges on the hinges. After a loud bang, the door fell open. The nine other SEALs rushed forward, ending up in an alleylike driveway with their backs to the house's main entrance. They moved down the alley, silenced rifles pressed against their shoulders. Mark hung toward the rear as he established radio communications with the other team. At the end of the driveway, the Americans blew through yet another locked gate and stepped into a courtyard facing the guesthouse, where Abu Ahmed al-Kuwaiti, bin Laden's courier, lived with his wife and four children.

Three SEALs in front broke off to clear the guesthouse as the remaining nine blasted through another gate and entered an inner courtyard, which faced the main house. When the smaller unit rounded the corner to face the doors of the guesthouse, they spotted Kuwaiti running inside to warn his wife and children. The

Americans' night-vision goggles cast the scene in pix-
elated shades of emerald green. Kuwaiti, wearing a white
shalwar kameez, had grabbed a weapon and was coming
back outside when the SEALs opened fire and killed him.

The nine other SEALs, including Mark, formed
three-man units for clearing the inner courtyard. The
Americans suspected that several more men were in the
house: Kuwaiti's thirty-three-year-old brother, Abrar; bin
Laden's sons Hamza and Khalid; and bin Laden himself.
One SEAL unit had no sooner trod on the paved patio
at the house's front entrance when Abrar—a stocky,
mustachioed man in a cream-colored shalwar kameez—
appeared with an AK-47. He was shot in the chest and
killed, as was his wife, Bushra, who was standing, unarmed, beside him.

Commotion in the Compound's Neighborhood

Outside the compound's walls, Ahmed, the translator,
patrolled the dirt road in front of bin Laden's house, as if
he were a plainclothes Pakistani police officer. He looked
the part, wearing a shalwar kameez atop a flak jacket.
He, the dog Cairo, and four SEALs
were responsible for closing off the
perimeter of the house while James
and six other SEALs—the contingent
that was supposed to have dropped
onto the roof—moved inside. For
the team patrolling the perimeter,
the first fifteen minutes passed without incident. Neighbors undoubtedly
heard the low-flying helicopters, the
sound of one crashing, and the spo-
radic explosions and gunfire that ensued, but nobody
came outside. One local took note of the tumult in a
Twitter post: "Helicopter hovering above Abbottabad at
1 AM (is a rare event)."

> The operation had been moni-
> tored by dozens of defense,
> intelligence, and Administration
> officials watching the drone's
> video feed.

Eventually, a few curious Pakistanis approached to inquire about the commotion on the other side of the wall. "Go back to your houses," Ahmed said, in Pashto, as Cairo stood watch. "There is a security operation under way." The locals went home, none of them suspecting that they had talked to an American. When journalists descended on Bilal Town in the coming days, one resident told a reporter, "I saw soldiers emerging from the helicopters and advancing toward the house. Some of them instructed us in chaste Pashto to turn off the lights and stay inside."

Meanwhile, James, the squadron commander, had breached one wall, crossed a section of the yard covered with trellises, breached a second wall, and joined up with the SEALs from helo one, who were entering the ground floor of the house. What happened next is not precisely clear. "I can tell you that there was a time period of almost twenty to twenty-five minutes where we really didn't know just exactly what was going on," [CIA director Leon] Panetta said later, on *PBS NewsHour*.

Until this moment, the operation had been monitored by dozens of defense, intelligence, and Administration officials watching the drone's video feed. The SEALs were not wearing helmet cams, contrary to a widely cited report by CBS. None of them had any previous knowledge of the house's floor plan, and they were further jostled by the awareness that they were possibly minutes away from ending the costliest manhunt in American history; as a result, some of their recollections—on which this account is based—may be imprecise and, thus, subject to dispute.

Clearing the House Room by Room

As Abrar's children ran for cover, the SEALs began clearing the first floor of the main house, room by room. Though the Americans had thought that the house might be booby-trapped, the presence of kids at the compound

A barrier hides parts of the remains of a crash-landed Navy SEAL helicopter near the Bin Laden compound in Abbottabad, Pakistan, on May 2, 2011. (© STR/AFP/ Getty Images.)

suggested otherwise. "You can only be hyper-vigilant for so long," the special-operations officer said. "Did bin Laden go to sleep every night thinking, The next night they're coming? Of course not. Maybe for the first year or two. But not now." Nevertheless, security precautions were in place. A locked metal gate blocked the base of the staircase leading to the second floor, making the downstairs room feel like a cage.

After blasting through the gate with C-4 charges, three SEALs marched up the stairs. Midway up, they saw bin Laden's twenty-three-year-old son, Khalid, craning his neck around the corner. He then appeared at the top of the staircase with an AK-47. Khalid, who wore a white T-shirt with an overstretched neckline and had short hair and a clipped beard, fired down at the Americans. (The counterterrorism official claims that Khalid was unarmed, though still a threat worth taking seriously.

> The first SEAL pushed [the bedroom door] open. Two of bin Laden's wives had placed themselves in front of him.

"You have an adult male, late at night, in the dark, coming down the stairs at you in an Al Qaeda house—your assumption is that you're encountering a hostile.") At least two of the SEALs shot back and killed Khalid. According to the booklets that the SEALs carried, up to five adult males were living inside the compound. Three of them were now dead; the fourth, bin Laden's son Hamza, was not on the premises. The final person was bin Laden.

Before the mission commenced, the SEALs had created a checklist of code words that had a Native American theme. Each code word represented a different stage of the mission: leaving Jalalabad, entering Pakistan, approaching the compound, and so on. "Geronimo" was to signify that bin Laden had been found.

Three SEALs shuttled past Khalid's body and blew open another metal cage, which obstructed the staircase leading to the third floor. Bounding up the unlit stairs, they scanned the railed landing. On the top stair, the lead SEAL swivelled right; with his night-vision goggles, he discerned that a tall, rangy man with a fist-length beard was peeking out from behind a bedroom door, ten feet away. The SEAL instantly sensed that it was Crankshaft [their code name for bin Laden]. (The counterterrorism official asserts that the SEAL first saw bin Laden on the landing, and fired but missed.)

The Americans hurried toward the bedroom door. The first SEAL pushed it open. Two of bin Laden's wives had placed themselves in front of him. Amal al-Fatah, bin Laden's fifth wife, was screaming in Arabic. She motioned as if she were going to charge; the SEAL lowered his sights and shot her once, in the calf. Fearing that one or both women were wearing suicide jackets, he stepped forward, wrapped them in a bear hug, and drove them aside. He would almost certainly have been killed had they blown themselves up, but by blanketing them he would have absorbed some of the blast and potentially saved the two SEALs behind him. In the end, neither woman was wearing an explosive vest.

A second SEAL stepped into the room and trained the infrared laser of his M4 on bin Laden's chest. The Al Qaeda chief, who was wearing a tan shalwar kameez and a prayer cap on his head, froze; he was unarmed. "There was never any question of detaining or capturing him—it wasn't a split-second decision. No one wanted detainees," the special-operations officer told me. (The Administration maintains that had bin Laden immediately surrendered he could have been taken alive.) Nine years, seven months, and twenty days after September 11th, an American was a trigger pull from ending bin Laden's life. The first round, a 5.56-mm. bullet, struck bin Laden in the chest. As he fell backward, the SEAL fired a second round into his head, just above his left eye. On his radio, he reported, "For God and country—Geronimo, Geronimo, Geronimo." After a pause, he added, "Geronimo E.K.I.A."—"enemy killed in action."

Hearing this at the White House, Obama pursed his lips, and said solemnly, to no one in particular, "We got him."

The Final Stages of the Raid

Relaxing his hold on bin Laden's two wives, the first SEAL placed the women in flex cuffs and led them downstairs. Two of his colleagues, meanwhile, ran upstairs with a nylon body bag. They unfurled it, knelt down on either side of bin Laden, and placed the body inside the bag. Eighteen minutes had elapsed since the DEVGRU team landed. For the next twenty minutes, the mission shifted to an intelligence-gathering operation.

Four men scoured the second floor, plastic bags in hand, collecting flash drives, CDs, DVDs, and computer hardware from the room, which had served, in part, as bin Laden's makeshift media studio. In the coming weeks, a C.I.A.-led task force examined the files and determined that bin Laden had remained far more involved in the operational activities of Al Qaeda than many American officials had thought. He had been developing plans to assassinate Obama and [General David] Petraeus, to pull off an extravagant September 11th anniversary attack, and to attack American trains. The SEALs also found an archive of digital pornography. "We find it on all these guys, whether they're in Somalia, Iraq, or Afghanistan," the special-operations officer said. Bin Laden's gold-threaded robes, worn during his video addresses, hung behind a curtain in the media room.

> A medic . . . injected a needle into bin Laden's body and extracted two bone-marrow samples. More DNA was taken with swabs.

Outside, the Americans corralled the women and children—each of them bound in flex cuffs—and had them sit against an exterior wall that faced the second, undamaged Black Hawk. The lone fluent Arabic speaker on the assault team questioned them. Nearly all the children were under the age of ten. They seemed to have no idea about the tenant upstairs, other than that he was "an old guy." None of the women confirmed that the man was bin Laden, though one of them kept referring to him as "the sheikh." When the rescue Chinook eventually arrived, a medic stepped out and knelt over the corpse. He injected a needle into bin Laden's body and extracted two bone-marrow samples. More DNA was taken with swabs. One of the bone-marrow samples went into the Black Hawk. The other went into the Chinook, along with bin Laden's body.

Next, the SEALs needed to destroy the damaged Black Hawk. The pilot, armed with a hammer that he kept for such situations, smashed the instrument panel, the radio, and the other classified fixtures inside the cockpit. Then the demolition unit took over. They placed explosives near the avionics system, the communications gear, the engine, and the rotor head. "You're not going to hide the fact that it's a helicopter," the special-operations officer said. "But you want to make it unusable." The SEALs placed extra C-4 charges under the carriage, rolled thermite grenades inside the copter's body, and then backed up. Helo one burst into flames while the demolition team boarded the Chinook. The women and children, who were being left behind for the Pakistani authorities, looked puzzled, scared, and shocked as they watched the SEALs board the helicopters. Amal, bin Laden's wife, continued her harangue. Then, as a giant fire burned inside the compound walls, the Americans flew away.

The US President Announces Bin Laden's Death

Barack Obama

The following viewpoint is the text of a televised speech given by President Barack Obama on May 2, 2011, announcing the assassination of Osama bin Laden. Obama begins by reminding viewers of the September 11, 2001, attacks and the destruction and heartbreak they caused as well as the unity experienced by the nation immediately after. The president states that as part of the ongoing war against the organization responsible for 9/11, he directed the CIA to prioritize the capture or killing of the al Qaeda leader. After announcing that Bin Laden had been killed by US forces in a targeted operation in Pakistan, the president states that the war against al Qaeda continues. He is careful to add that the United States is not at war against Islam and to thank all who continue to serve in the war on terror. Barack Obama is the forty-fourth president of the United States.

SOURCE. Barack Obama, "Remarks by the President on Osama Bin Laden," The White House, May 2, 2011.

Good evening. Tonight, I can report to the American people and to the world that the United States has conducted an operation that killed Osama bin Laden, the leader of al Qaeda, and a terrorist who's responsible for the murder of thousands of innocent men, women, and children.

It was nearly 10 years ago that a bright September day was darkened by the worst attack on the American people in our history. The images of 9/11 are seared into our national memory—hijacked planes cutting through a cloudless September sky; the Twin Towers collapsing to the ground; black smoke billowing up from the Pentagon; the wreckage of Flight 93 in Shanksville, Pennsylvania, where the actions of heroic citizens saved even more heartbreak and destruction.

> " We went to war against al Qaeda to protect our citizens, our friends, and our allies. "

And yet we know that the worst images are those that were unseen to the world. The empty seat at the dinner table. Children who were forced to grow up without their mother or their father. Parents who would never know the feeling of their child's embrace. Nearly 3,000 citizens taken from us, leaving a gaping hole in our hearts.

On September 11, 2001, in our time of grief, the American people came together. We offered our neighbors a hand, and we offered the wounded our blood. We reaffirmed our ties to each other, and our love of community and country. On that day, no matter where we came from, what God we prayed to, or what race or ethnicity we were, we were united as one American family.

We were also united in our resolve to protect our nation and to bring those who committed this vicious attack to justice. We quickly learned that the 9/11 attacks were carried out by al Qaeda—an organization headed by Osama bin Laden, which had openly declared war on the United States and was committed to killing innocents in our country and around the globe. And so we went to war against al Qaeda to protect our citizens, our friends, and our allies.

Over the last 10 years, thanks to the tireless and heroic work of our military and our counterterrorism professionals, we've made great strides in that effort. We've disrupted terrorist attacks and strengthened our homeland defense. In Afghanistan, we removed the Taliban government, which had given bin Laden and al Qaeda safe haven and support. And around the globe, we worked with our friends and allies to capture or kill scores of al Qaeda terrorists, including several who were a part of the 9/11 plot.

Catching bin Laden Was a Priority

Yet Osama bin Laden avoided capture and escaped across the Afghan border into Pakistan. Meanwhile, al Qaeda continued to operate from along that border and operate through its affiliates across the world.

And so shortly after taking office, I directed Leon Panetta, the director of the CIA, to make the killing or capture of bin Laden the top priority of our war against al Qaeda, even as we continued our broader efforts to disrupt, dismantle, and defeat his network.

Then, last August [2010], after years of painstaking work by our intelligence community, I was briefed on a possible lead to bin Laden. It was far from certain, and it took many months to run this thread to ground. I met repeatedly with my national security team as we developed more information about the possibility that we had located bin Laden hiding within a compound deep inside of Pakistan. And finally, last week, I determined that we had enough intelligence to take action, and authorized an operation to get Osama bin Laden and bring him to justice.

Today, at my direction, the United States launched a targeted operation against that compound in Abbot-

tabad, Pakistan. A small team of Americans carried out the operation with extraordinary courage and capability. No Americans were harmed. They took care to avoid civilian casualties. After a firefight, they killed Osama bin Laden and took custody of his body.

US president Barack Obama announces the assassination of Osama bin Laden in a televised speech from the White House on May 2, 2011. (© Chris Kleponis/AFP/Getty Image.)

For over two decades, bin Laden has been al Qaeda's leader and symbol, and has continued to plot attacks against our country and our friends and allies. The death of bin Laden marks the most significant achievement to date in our nation's effort to defeat al Qaeda.

The Fight Against al Qaeda Continues

Yet his death does not mark the end of our effort. There's no doubt that al Qaeda will continue to pursue attacks against us. We must—and we will—remain vigilant at home and abroad.

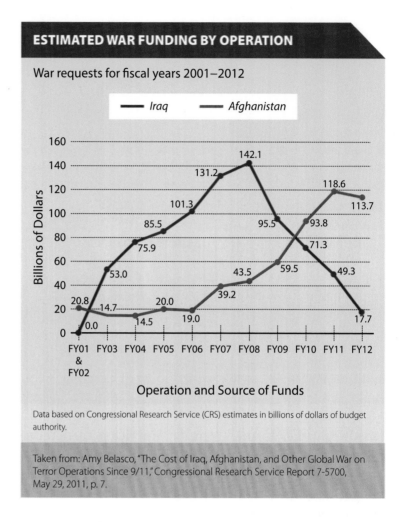

ESTIMATED WAR FUNDING BY OPERATION

War requests for fiscal years 2001–2012

— Iraq   — Afghanistan

Operation and Source of Funds

Data based on Congressional Research Service (CRS) estimates in billions of dollars of budget authority.

Taken from: Amy Belasco, "The Cost of Iraq, Afghanistan, and Other Global War on Terror Operations Since 9/11," Congressional Research Service Report 7-5700, May 29, 2011, p. 7.

As we do, we must also reaffirm that the United States is not—and never will be—at war with Islam. I've made clear, just as President [George W.] Bush did shortly after 9/11, that our war is not against Islam. Bin Laden was not a Muslim leader; he was a mass murderer of Muslims. Indeed, al Qaeda has slaughtered scores of Muslims in many countries, including our own. So his demise should be welcomed by all who believe in peace and human dignity.

Over the years, I've repeatedly made clear that we would take action within Pakistan if we knew where bin

Laden was. That is what we've done. But it's important to note that our counterterrorism cooperation with Pakistan helped lead us to bin Laden and the compound where he was hiding. Indeed, bin Laden had declared war against Pakistan as well, and ordered attacks against the Pakistani people.

Tonight, I called President [of Pakistan Asif Ali] Zardari, and my team has also spoken with their Pakistani counterparts. They agree that this is a good and historic day for both of our nations. And going forward, it is essential that Pakistan continue to join us in the fight against al Qaeda and its affiliates.

The American people did not choose this fight. It came to our shores, and started with the senseless slaughter of our citizens. After nearly 10 years of service, struggle, and sacrifice, we know well the costs of war. These efforts weigh on me every time I, as Commander-in-Chief, have to sign a letter to a family that has lost a loved one, or look into the eyes of a service member who's been gravely wounded.

> Justice has been done.

So Americans understand the costs of war. Yet as a country, we will never tolerate our security being threatened, nor stand idly by when our people have been killed. We will be relentless in defense of our citizens and our friends and allies. We will be true to the values that make us who we are. And on nights like this one, we can say to those families who have lost loved ones to al Qaeda's terror: Justice has been done.

Expressing Gratitude for All Who Have Worked for Justice

Tonight, we give thanks to the countless intelligence and counterterrorism professionals who've worked tirelessly to achieve this outcome. The American people do not see their work, nor know their names. But tonight, they feel the satisfaction of their work and the result of their pursuit of justice.

We give thanks for the men who carried out this operation, for they exemplify the professionalism, patriotism, and unparalleled courage of those who serve our country. And they are part of a generation that has borne the heaviest share of the burden since that September day.

Finally, let me say to the families who lost loved ones on 9/11 that we have never forgotten your loss, nor wavered in our commitment to see that we do whatever it takes to prevent another attack on our shores.

And tonight, let us think back to the sense of unity that prevailed on 9/11. I know that it has, at times, frayed. Yet today's achievement is a testament to the greatness of our country and the determination of the American people.

The cause of securing our country is not complete. But tonight, we are once again reminded that America can do whatever we set our mind to. That is the story of our history, whether it's the pursuit of prosperity for our people, or the struggle for equality for all our citizens; our commitment to stand up for our values abroad, and our sacrifices to make the world a safer place.

Let us remember that we can do these things not just because of wealth or power, but because of who we are: one nation, under God, indivisible, with liberty and justice for all.

Thank you. May God bless you. And may God bless the United States of America.

Pakistan's Parliament Condemns the Raid

Senate of Pakistan and National Assembly

The following viewpoint is the text of a resolution adopted by the Parliament of Pakistan in a joint session of the Senate and National Assembly. (Pakistan is a federal republic with a bicameral legislature, similar to the government of the United States.) The legislature states that it reviewed the US actions related to the raid on the Bin Laden compound in Abbottabad, Pakistan, and found them to be in violation of Pakistani sovereignty. The legislature claims that the raid, as well as other US armed forces activity in Pakistan, was unacceptable and in violation of international law. The government expresses distress that its efforts and sacrifices in the war against terror have not been properly acknowledged by the international community. As a result, the resolution states, the government will review the terms of its relationship with the United States and establish a special commission to investigate the Bin Laden raid.

SOURCE. Senate of Pakistan and National Assembly, "Resolution Adopted by the Joint Session of Parliament," Government of Pakistan, July 10, 2013.

The Senate of Pakistan and the National Assembly, in a Joint Session held on 13–14 May 2011, considered the situation arising from the unilateral US forces action in Abbottabad on 2 May 2011.

After an in-depth discussion, including presentations made on the relevant issues by the Director General, Inter-Services Intelligence, Director General Military Operations and Deputy Chief of Air Staff Operations, the Joint Session of Parliament resolved as under:

Condemned the US unilateral action in Abbottabad, which constitutes a violation of Pakistan's sovereignty;

Strongly asserted that unilateral actions, such as those conducted by the US forces in Abbottabad, as well as the continued drone attacks on the territory of Pakistan, are not only unacceptable but also constitute violation of the principles of the Charter of the United Nations, international law and humanitarian norms and such drone attacks must be stopped forthwith, failing which the Government will be constrained to consider taking necessary steps including withdrawal of transit facility allowed to NATO/ISAF forces;

> [Pakistan] expressed its deep distress on the campaign to malign Pakistan . . . without appreciating [its] determined efforts and immense sacrifices in combating terror.

Determines that unilateral actions cannot advance the global cause of elimination of terrorism, and the people of Pakistan will no longer tolerate such actions and repeat of unilateral measures could have dire consequences for peace and security in the region and the world.

Reaffirmed the resolve of the people and Government of Pakistan to uphold Pakistan's sovereignty and national security, which is a sacred duty, at all costs;

Affirmed the resolve of the people and state institutions of Pakistan to safeguard Pakistan's national interests and strategic assets and, in this context, underscored that any action to the contrary will warrant a strong national response;

Expressed its deep distress on the campaign to malign Pakistan, launched by certain quarters in other countries without appreciating Pakistan's determined efforts and immense sacrifices in combating terror and the fact that more than thirty thousand Pakistani innocent men, women and children and more than five thousand security and armed forces personnel had lost their lives, that is more than any other single country, in the fight against terror and the blowback emanating from actions of the NATO/ISAF forces in Afghanistan;

Pakistani prime minister Yousuf Raza Gilani addresses Parliament on May 9, 2011, about Osama bin Laden's presence in the country during a session in which the government condemned the US raid. (© Yslb Pak/ ZUMAPRESS/Newscom.)

Called upon the Government to ensure that the principles of an independent foreign policy must be grounded

in strict adherence to the principles of policy, as stated in Article 40 of the Constitution, the UN Charter, observance of international law and respect for the free will and aspirations of sovereign states and their peoples;

Further Called upon the Government to re-visit and review its terms of engagement with the United States, with a view to ensuring that Pakistan's national interests are fully respected and accommodated in pursuit of policies for countering terrorism and achieving reconciliation and peace in Afghanistan;

Affirmed the importance of international cooperation for eliminating international terrorism, which can only be carried forward on the basis of a true partnership approach, based on equality, mutual respect and mutual trust;

Affirmed Also full confidence in the defence forces of Pakistan in safeguarding Pakistan's sovereignty, independence and territorial integrity and in overcoming any challenge to security, with the full support of the people and Government of Pakistan. . . .

Called upon the Government to appoint an independent Commission on the Abbottabad operation, fix responsibility and recommend necessary measures to ensure that such an incident does not recur. The composition/ modalities of the Commission will be settled after consultations between the Leader of the House and the Leader of the Opposition.

The Abbottabad Commission Report Is Leaked to the Media

South Asian Media Network

In 2011 the parliament of Pakistan issued a resolution to investigate Osama bin Laden's assassination. The result was the *Abbottabad Commission Report*, which the Pakistani government chose not to release publicly, according to the news story in the following viewpoint. The viewpoint states that the report was released by the news organization Al Jazeera, which concluded that the report was commissioned so that the government could distance itself from the embarrassment of the raid. The report, according to the viewpoint, is highly critical of the civilian and military leadership, finding that the government's response to both the search for Bin Laden and the US raid was negligent and incompetent. The report also contains new details about the raid, including testimony from Bin Laden's family. The South Asian Media Network is an independent news website that provides coverage of news from

Bangladesh, India, Pakistan, Afghanistan, Sri Lanka, Nepal, Maldives, and Bhutan.

According to a copy of Abbottabad Commission Report, July 10 [2013]—acquired by a media outlet—no institution or individual was aware of former al-Qaeda leader, Osama bin Laden's, presence in Pakistan.

According to report the US Navy SEALS were provided with strategic ground support for the operation to capture world's most wanted man. The report reveals the sequence of events that helped United States of America hunt down world's most wanted man.

The report says the statements of President Asif Ali Zardari, former Prime Minister Yousuf Raza Gilani, and Chief of the Army Staff, General Ashfaq Parvez Kayani remain reserved to date as they did not appear before the commission. The testimonies of Osama's wives are also a part of the report. The commission also reported that tracing Osama Bin Laden in Pakistan and subsequently sharing this intelligence with the government was solely Inter Services Intelligence's (ISI) responsibility. Al Jazeera says the report calls the handling of bin Laden affair a "national disgrace."

> [The] Pakistani government report . . . blasts the country's civilian and military leadership for 'gross incompetence' over the bin Laden affair.

Pakistan Accused of "Gross Incompetence"

Osama bin Laden lived undetected in Pakistan for nine years before he was killed by U.S. forces according to leaked Pakistani government report that blasts the country's civilian and military leadership for "gross incompetence" over the bin Laden affair. It finds that Pakistan's intelligence establishment had "closed the book" on bin Laden by 2005, and was no longer actively pursuing intelligence that could lead to his capture.

The 336-page Abbottabad Commission report, obtained by Al Jazeera, blasts the government and military for a "national disaster" over its handling of bin Laden and calls on the leadership to apologize to the people of Pakistan for their "dereliction of duty." The report, never released publicly, was ordered after the May 1, 2011 raid by U.S. special forces on bin Laden's compound in Abbottabad. The al-Qaeda leader was killed and his body removed during the raid.

According to Al Jazeera, the report finds the government's intention in conducting the inquiry was likely aimed at "regime continuance, when the regime is desperate to distance itself from any responsibility for the national disaster that occurred on its watch." It says that the inquiry was likely "a reluctant response to an overwhelming public and parliamentary demand." The report blames "Government Implosion Syndrome" for lack of intelligence on Bin Laden's nine-year residence in

Justice Javed Iqbal (center) leads a meeting of the Abbottabad Commission in 2011. (© PPI/ ZUMAPRESS/Newscom.)

> '[Bin Laden] did not use his wife or daughter as a shield to protect himself,' the report says.

Pakistan and its response to the U.S. raid.

Al Jazeera quotes the report as saying the commissions finds that "culpable negligence and incompetence at almost all levels of government can more or less be conclusively established." The reports focuses intently on the night of the raid, interviewing bin Laden's family and members of the household extensively.

Accounts About the Raid

The report said accounts differ as to whether the al-Qaeda leader was killed by the first shot fired at him when he went to the bedroom door as soldiers came up the stairs or later when they stormed the room.

Pakistani police stand guard beside a sealed main gate leading to the hideout house of slain al-Qaeda leader Osama bin Laden in Abbottabad on May 4, 2011. "He did not use his wife or daughter as a shield to protect himself," the report says. "He was not armed when he was shot."

One of his daughters, identified as Surnayya, told the commission that she saw one of the U.S. helicopters land from her window and immediately rushed upstairs to bin Laden's room.

"Although she did not see her father fall, she saw him on the floor," the report says. "He had been hit in the forehead and she knew he was dead. His face was 'clear' and recognizable. According to her, blood flowed 'backwards over his head.' However, because of the dark she could not see very clearly. The American soldiers asked her to identify the body. She said, 'my father.'"

The Report's Main Findings

In summing up its assessment of the killing of bin Laden, the commission spares few words: The whole episode of the U.S. assassination mission of May 2, 2011 and the Pakistan government's response before, during and after appears in large part to be a story of complacency, ignorance, negligence, incompetence, irresponsibility and possibly worse at various levels inside and outside the government. Among other findings:

- Bin Laden entered Pakistan in mid-2002 after narrowly escaping capture in the battle of Tora Bora in Afghanistan. Over nine years, he moved to various places inside the country, including South Waziristan and northern Swat Valley.

- In Swat, the al-Qaeda leader reportedly met with Khalid Shaikh Mohammad [KSM], the alleged mastermind of the 9/11 attacks, in early 2003. About a month later, KSM was captured in Rawalpindi in a joint U.S.-Pakistani operation, and Bin Laden fled the area.

- Bin Laden, along with two of his wives and several children and grandchildren, moved into the custom-built compound in Abbottabad, a military garrison town, in 2005 and lived there until the U.S. raid.

- The presence of a CIA support network to help track down bin Laden without the Pakistani establishment's knowledge was "a case of nothing less than a collective and sustained dereliction of duty by the political, military and intelligence leadership of the country."

CHAPTER 2

Controversies Surrounding the Assassination of Osama bin Laden

Harsh Interrogation Techniques Helped the United States Find Bin Laden

Michael B. Mukasey

In the following viewpoint, the author claims the intelligence that eventually led to Osama bin Laden's assassination was facilitated by harsh interrogation techniques. Specifically he points to information provided by Khalid Sheik Mohammed and other men with ties to al Qaeda who were interrogated using the techniques. He criticizes the Barack Obama administration for pledging to do away with the techniques and for disclosing them to the public. He argues that the interrogation techniques were legal, fruitful, and important, and they should have remained secret. Michael B. Mukasey is a former lawyer and judge who served as attorney general of the United States from 2007 to 2009.

Photo on opposite page: Pakistani Islamists protest the killing of Osama bin Laden at a May 2011 demonstration. Critics in the Middle East and the West question whether the assassination was legal or prudent. (© **Banaras Khan/AFP/Getty Images.**)

SOURCE. Michael B. Mukasey, "The Waterboarding Trail to bin Laden," *Wall Street Journal*, May 6, 2011. Copyright © 2011 by Michael B. Mukasey. All rights reserved. Reproduced by permission.

Osama bin Laden was killed by Americans, based on intelligence developed by Americans. That should bring great satisfaction to our citizens and elicit praise for our intelligence community. Seized along with bin Laden's corpse was a trove of documents and electronic devices that should yield intelligence that could help us capture or kill other terrorists and further degrade the capabilities of those who remain at large.

But policies put in place by the very administration that presided over this splendid success promise fewer such successes in the future. Those policies make it unlikely that we'll be able to get information from those whose identities are disclosed by the material seized from bin Laden. The administration also hounds our intelligence gatherers in ways that can only demoralize them.

The Trail to bin Laden Begins with KSM

Consider how the intelligence that led to bin Laden came to hand. It began with a disclosure from Khalid Sheikh Mohammed (KSM), who broke like a dam under the pressure of harsh interrogation techniques that included waterboarding. He loosed a torrent of information—including eventually the nickname of a trusted courier of bin Laden.

> Members of al Qaeda were obligated to resist [interrogation] only until they could no longer do so.

That regimen of harsh interrogation was used on KSM after another detainee, Abu Zubaydeh, was subjected to the same techniques. When he broke, he said that he and other members of al Qaeda were obligated to resist only until they could no longer do so, at which point it became permissible for them to yield. "Do this for all the brothers," he advised his interrogators.

Abu Zubaydeh was coerced into disclosing information that led to the capture of Ramzi bin al Shibh,

Who Is Khalid Sheikh Mohammed?

Since June, 2002, when U.S. officials first identified [Khalid Sheikh] Mohammed as the "mastermind" of 9/11, he has become one of history's most famous criminals. Yet, unlike Osama bin Laden, he has remained essentially unknown. Efforts to uncover more than the outlines of his biography have produced sketchy and sometimes contradictory results. . . . Even basic facts have been in doubt; there are, for example, at least three versions of his birth date. For almost the entire decade before he was captured, in early 2003, Mohammed was a fugitive, deliberately obscuring his tracks. Bin Laden, meanwhile, was hosting television interviewers, giving speeches, and distributing videos and text versions of his proclamations to whoever would have them.

Insofar as we know Mohammed, we see him as a brilliant behind-the-scenes tactician and a resolute ideologue. As it turns out, he is earthy, slick in a way, but naive, and seemingly motivated as much by pathology as by ideology. [Al Jazeera reporter Yosri] Fouda describes Mohammed's Arabic as crude and colloquial and his knowledge of Islamic texts as almost nonexistent. A journalist who observed Mohammed's appearance at one of the Guantanamo hearings likened his voluble performance to that of a Pakistani Jackie Mason [an American comedian]. A college classmate said that he was an eager participant in impromptu skits and plays. A man who knew him from a mosque in Doha talked about his quick wit and chatty, glad-handing style. He was an operator.

In at least one important way, though, his boasts are accurate. Mohammed, not Osama bin Laden, was the essential figure in the 9/11 plot. The attacks were his idea, carried out under his direct command. Mohammed has said that he went so far as to resist swearing allegiance to bin Laden and Al Qaeda until after the attacks, so that he could continue pursuing them if Al Qaeda lost courage.

SOURCE. Terry McDermott, "The Mastermind," New Yorker, September 13, 2010.

another of the planners of 9/11. Bin al Shibh disclosed information that, when combined with what was learned from Abu Zubaydeh, helped lead to the capture of KSM and other senior terrorists and the disruption of follow-on plots aimed at both Europe and the United States.

Another of those gathered up later in this harvest, Abu Faraj al-Libi, also was subjected to certain of these harsh techniques and disclosed further details about bin Laden's couriers that helped in last weekend's [May 2011] achievement.

Harsh Interrogation Was Used Selectively

The harsh techniques themselves were used selectively against only a small number of hardcore prisoners who successfully resisted other forms of interrogation, and then only with the explicit authorization of the director of the CIA. Of the thousands of unlawful combatants captured by the U.S., fewer than 100 were detained and questioned in the CIA program. Of those, fewer than one-third were subjected to any of these techniques.

Former CIA Director Michael Hayden has said that, as late as 2006, even with the growing success of other intelligence tools, fully half of the government's knowledge about the structure and activities of al Qaeda came from those interrogations. The [George W.] Bush administration put these techniques in place only after rigorous analysis by the Justice Department, which concluded that they were lawful. Regrettably, that same administration gave them a name—"enhanced interrogation techniques"—so absurdly antiseptic as to imply that it must conceal something unlawful.

The Obama Administration's Missteps

The current president ran for election on the promise to do away with them even before he became aware, if he ever did, of what they were. Days after taking office he directed that the CIA interrogation program be done away with entirely, and that interrogation be limited to the techniques set forth in the Army Field

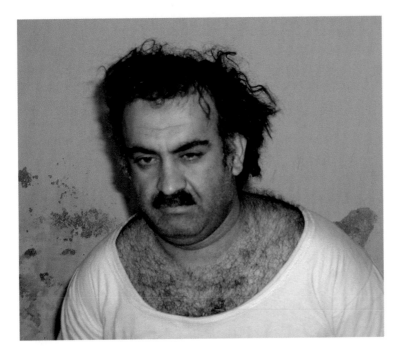

Khalid Sheikh Mohammed is captured by US forces in Pakistan in 2003. He provided information to investigators while being subjected to enhanced interrogation techniques. (© AP Images.)

Manual, a document designed for use by even the least experienced troops. It's available on the Internet and used by terrorists as a training manual for resisting interrogation.

In April 2009, the administration made public the previously classified Justice Department memoranda analyzing the harsh techniques, thereby disclosing them to our enemies and assuring that they could never be used effectively again. Meanwhile, the administration announced its intentions to replace the CIA interrogation program with one administered by the FBI. In December 2009, Omar Faruq Abdulmutallab was caught in an airplane over Detroit trying to detonate a bomb concealed in his underwear. He was warned after apprehension of his Miranda rights, and it was later disclosed that no one had yet gotten around to implementing the new program.

Yet the Justice Department, revealing its priorities, had gotten around to reopening investigations into the

> "The techniques are neither dirty nor . . . were their results little."

conduct of a half dozen CIA employees alleged to have used undue force against suspected terrorists. I say "reopening" advisedly because those investigations had all been formally closed by the end of 2007, with detailed memoranda prepared by career Justice Department prosecutors explaining why no charges were warranted. Attorney General Eric Holder conceded that he had ordered the investigations reopened in September 2009 without reading those memoranda. The investigations have now dragged on for years with prosecutors chasing allegations down rabbit holes, with the CIA along with the rest of the intelligence community left demoralized.

Not a "Dirty Little Secret"

Immediately following the killing of bin Laden, the issue of interrogation techniques became in some quarters the "dirty little secret" of the event. But as disclosed in the declassified memos in 2009, the techniques are neither dirty nor, as noted by Director Hayden and others, were their results little. As the memoranda concluded—and as I concluded reading them at the beginning of my tenure as attorney general in 2007—the techniques were entirely lawful as the law stood at the time the memos were written, and the disclosures they elicited were enormously important. That they are no longer secret is deeply regrettable.

It is debatable whether the same techniques would be lawful under statutes passed in 2005 and 2006—phrased in highly abstract terms such as "cruel, inhuman and degrading" treatment—that some claimed were intended to ban waterboarding even though the Senate twice voted down proposals to ban the technique specifically. It is, however, certain that intelligence gathering rather than prosecution must be the first priority, and that we need a classified interrogation program administered by the agency best equipped to administer it: the CIA.

We also need to put an end to the ongoing investigations of CIA operatives that continue to undermine intelligence community morale.

Acknowledging and meeting the need for an effective and lawful interrogation program, which we once had, and freeing CIA operatives and others to administer it under congressional oversight, would be a fitting way to mark the demise of Osama bin Laden.

Harsh Interrogation Techniques Are Ineffective and Immoral

John McCain

The following viewpoint consists of a US senator's remarks in Congress shortly after the announcement that Osama bin Laden had been killed. The senator delivers an impassioned critique of harsh interrogation techniques, which he says are "indisputably torture" and illegal. He specifically criticizes statements by government officials that useful information in the search for Bin Laden was obtained using such techniques. In truth, he says, the information obtained was false and misleading. More important, he argues, is the fact that torture is contrary to American values and morals—to the very ideals the country is fighting for in the war against terror. John McCain has represented the state of Arizona in the US Senate since 1987 and was the Republican candidate for US president in 2008. He was severely tortured and left with permanent injuries as a prisoner of war in North Vietnam from 1967 to 1973.

SOURCE. John McCain, "Use of Torture," Congressional Record, May 12, 2011.

The successful end of the 10-year manhunt to bring Osama bin Laden to justice has appropriately heightened the Nation's appreciation for the diligence, patriotism, and courage of our Armed Forces and our intelligence community. They are a great credit and inspiration to the country that has asked so much of them and, like all Americans, I am in their debt.

But their success has also reignited debate over whether the so-called enhanced interrogation techniques of enemy prisoners, including waterboarding, were instrumental in locating bin Laden and whether they are necessary and justifiable means for securing valuable information that might help prevent future terrorist attacks against us and our allies and lead to the capture or killing of those who would perpetrate them. Or are they, and should they be, prohibited by our conscience and laws as torture or cruel, inhuman, and degrading treatment.

> "I opposed . . . so-called enhanced interrogation techniques before Osama bin Laden was brought to justice, and I oppose them now."

I believe some of these practices—especially waterboarding, which is a mock execution, and thus to me indisputably torture—are and should be prohibited in a nation that is exceptional in its defense and advocacy of human rights. I believe they are a violation of the Detainee Treatment Act of 2005, the Military Commissions Act of 2006, and Common Article Three of the Geneva Conventions, all of which forbid cruel, inhuman, and degrading treatment of all captured combatants, whether they wear the uniform of a country or are essentially stateless.

Torture Is Not Necessary and Will Backfire

I opposed waterboarding and similar so-called enhanced interrogation techniques before Osama bin Laden was brought to justice, and I oppose them now. I do not believe they are necessary to our success in our war against terrorists, as the advocates of these techniques claim they are.

Even more importantly, I believe that if America uses torture, it could someday result in the torture of American combatants. Yes, I know al-Qaida and other terrorist organizations do not share our scruples about the treatment of enemy combatants, and have and will continue to subject American soldiers and anyone they capture to the cruelest mistreatment imaginable. But we must bear in mind the likelihood that someday we will be involved in a more conventional war against a state and not a terrorist movement or insurgency and be careful that we do not set a standard that another country could use to justify their mistreatment of our prisoners.

Lastly, it is difficult to overstate the damage that any practice of torture or cruel, inhuman, and degrading treatment by Americans does to our national character and historical reputation—to our standing as an exceptional nation among the countries of the world. It is too grave to justify the use of these interrogation techniques. America has made its progress in the world not only by avidly pursuing our geopolitical interests, but by persuading and inspiring other nations to embrace the political values that distinguish us. As I have said many times before, and still maintain, this is not about the terrorists. It is about us.

I understand the reasons that govern the decision to approve these interrogation methods, and I know those who approved them and those who employed them in the interrogation of captured terrorists were admirably dedicated to protecting the American people from harm. I know they were determined to keep faith with the victims of terrorism and to prove to our enemies that the United States would pursue justice tirelessly, relentlessly, and successfully, no matter how long it took. I know their responsibilities were grave and urgent, and the strain of their duty was considerable. I admire their dedication and love of country. But I dispute that it was right to use these methods, which I do not believe were in the best interests of justice or our security or the ideals that define us and which we have sacrificed much to defend. . . .

I do not believe anyone should be prosecuted for having used these techniques in the past, and I agree that the administration should state definitively that no one will be. As one of the authors of the Military Commissions Act, which I believe prohibits waterboarding and other "enhanced interrogation techniques," we wrote into the language of the law that no one who used them before the enactment of the law should be prosecuted. I do not think it is helpful or wise to revisit that policy.

Torturing Khalid Sheikh Mohammed Did Not Lead to bin Laden

Many advocates of these techniques have asserted their use on terrorists in our custody, particularly Khalid Sheikh Mohammed, revealed the trail to bin Laden—a trail which had gone cold in recent years but would now lead to his destruction. The former Attorney General of the United States, Michael Mukasey, recently claimed that "the intelligence that led to bin Laden . . . began with a disclosure from Khalid Sheikh Mohammed, who broke like a dam under the pressure of harsh interrogation techniques that included waterboarding. He loosed a torrent of information—including eventually the nickname of a trusted courier of bin Laden." That is false.

With so much misinformation being fed into such an essential public debate as this one, I asked the Director of Central Intelligence, Leon Panetta, for the facts, and I received the following information:

The trail to bin Laden did not begin with a disclosure from Khalid Sheikh Mohammed, who was waterboarded 183 times. We did not first learn from Khalid Sheikh

Mohammed the real name of bin Laden's courier, or his alias, Abu Ahmed al-Kuwaiti—the man who ultimately enabled us to find bin Laden. The first mention of the name Abu Ahmed al-Kuwaiti, as well as a description of him as an important member of al-Qaida, came from a detainee held in another country. The United States did not conduct this detainee's interrogation, nor did we render him to that country for the purpose of interrogation. We did not learn Abu Ahmed's real name or alias as a result of waterboarding or any "enhanced interrogation technique" used on a detainee in U.S. custody.

None of the three detainees who were waterboarded provided Abu Ahmed's real name, his whereabouts, or an accurate description of his role in al-Qaida.

> It was not torture or cruel, inhuman, and degrading treatment of detainees that got us the major leads that ultimately [found] Osama bin Laden.

In fact, not only did the use of "enhanced interrogation techniques" on Khalid Sheikh Mohammed not provide us with key leads on bin Laden's courier, Abu Ahmed, it actually produced false and misleading information. Khalid Sheikh Mohammed specifically told his interrogators that Abu Ahmed had moved to Peshawar, got married, and ceased his role as an al-Qaida facilitator—which was not true, as we now know. All we learned about Abu Ahmed al-Kuwaiti through the use of waterboarding and other "enhanced interrogation techniques" against Khalid Sheikh Mohammed was the confirmation of the already known fact that the courier existed and used an alias.

I have sought further information from the staff of the Senate Intelligence Committee, and they confirmed for me that, in fact, the best intelligence gained from a CIA detainee—information describing Abu Ahmed al-Kuwaiti's real role in al-Qaida and his true relationship to Osama bin Laden—was obtained through standard, noncoercive means, not through any "enhanced inter-rogation technique."

In short, it was not torture or cruel, inhuman, and degrading treatment of detainees that got us the major leads that ultimately enabled our intelligence commu-nity to find Osama bin Laden. I hope former Attorney General Mukasey will correct his misstatement. It is important that he do so because we are again engaged in this important debate, with much at stake for America's security and reputation. Each side should make its own case but do so without making up its own facts. . . .

Torture Is a Moral Issue

Ultimately, this is about morality. What is at stake is the very idea of America—the America whose values have

Activists stage a demonstration of waterboarding dur-ing a 2007 protest in Washington, DC, against the govern-ment's use of torture techniques. (© Mark Wilson/Getty Images.)

Enhanced Interrogation Techniques Are Contrary to American Values

The following remarks were delivered by President Barack Obama during a press conference on August 1, 2014. His statement was prompted by reporters' questions after a study by the US Senate Intelligence Committee of the CIA's Rendition/Detention/Interrogation (RDI) program was made public.

Even before I came into office I was very clear that in the immediate aftermath of 9/11 we did some things that were wrong. We did a whole lot of things that were right, but we tortured some folks. We did some things that were contrary to our values.

I understand why it happened. I think it's important when we look back to recall how afraid people were after the Twin Towers fell and the Pentagon had been hit and the plane in Pennsylvania had fallen, and people did not know whether more attacks were imminent, and there was enormous pressure on our law enforcement and our national security teams to try to deal with this. And it's important for us not to feel too sanctimonious in retrospect about the tough job that those folks had. And a lot of those folks were working hard under enormous pressure and are real patriots.

But having said all that, we did some things that were wrong. . . . And that's the reason why, after I took office, one of the first things I did was to ban some of the extraordinary interrogation techniques. . . .

The character of our country has to be measured in part not by what we do when things are easy, but what we do when things are hard. And when we engaged in some of these enhanced interrogation techniques, techniques that I believe and I think any fair-minded person would believe were torture, we crossed a line. . . . That needs to be understood and accepted. And we have to, as a country, take responsibility for that so that, hopefully, we don't do it again in the future.

SOURCE. *Barack Obama, "Press Conference by the President," August 1, 2014. Office of the Press Secretary, The White House. www.whitehouse.gov.*

inspired the world and instilled in the hearts of its citizens the certainty that no matter how hard we fight, no matter how dangerous our adversary, in the course of vanquishing our enemies, we do not compromise our deepest values. We are America, and we hold our our-selves to a higher standard. That is what is at stake.

Although Osama bin Laden is dead, America re-mains at war, and to prevail in this war we need more than victories on the battlefield. This is a war of ideas as well, a struggle to advance freedom in the face of terror in places where oppressive rule has bred the malevolence that feeds the ideology of violent extremism. Prisoner abuses exact a terrible toll on us in this war of ideas. They inevitably become public, and when they do they threaten our moral standard and expose us to false but widely dis-seminated charges that democracies are no more inherently idealistic and moral than other regimes.

> When we fight to defend our security, we also fight for an idea . . . that all men are endowed by their Creator with inalienable rights.

I understand that Islamic extrem-ists who resort to terror would de-stroy us utterly if they could obtain the weapons to do so. But to defeat them utterly, we must also prevail in our defense of the universal values that ultimately have the greatest power to eradicate this evil ideology. . . .

Individuals might forfeit their life and liberty as pun-ishment for breaking laws, but even then, as recognized in our Constitution's prohibition of cruel and unusual punishment, they are still entitled to respect for their basic human dignity, even if they have denied that re-spect to others.

I do not mourn the loss of any terrorist's life, nor do I care if in the course of serving their malevolent cause they suffer great harm. They have earned their terrible punishment in this life and the next. What I do mourn is what we lose when by official policy or official neglect we allow, confuse, or encourage those who fight this war for us to forget that best sense of ourselves, that which is our greatest strength; that when we fight to defend our security, we also fight for an idea, not a tribe, not a land, not a king, not a twisted interpretation of an ancient religion, but for an idea that all men are endowed by their Creator with inalienable rights.

It is indispensable to our success in this war that those we ask to fight it know that in the discharge of their dangerous responsibilities to our country, they are never expected to forget they are Americans and the valiant defenders of a sacred idea of how nations should be governed and conduct their relations with others—even our enemies.

Those of us who have given them this onerous duty are obliged by our history and the many terrible sacrifices that have been made in our defense to make clear to them that they need not risk our country's honor to prevail, that they are always—through the violence, chaos, and heartache of war, through deprivation, cruelty and loss, they are always Americans, and different, stronger, and better than those who would destroy us.

Who Actually Killed Bin Laden Is Unclear

Rupert Cornwell

The following viewpoint reports on the differing and somewhat contradictory accounts of the events at the Bin Laden compound during the Navy SEAL raid in 2011. The viewpoint states that confusion began immediately, with statements made by the White House about the raid. The identity of the shooter seemed to be settled when *No Easy Day*, a 2012 book by a former SEAL, was published. However the identity of the shooter was contradicted a few months later by a profile in *Esquire* magazine. That account was almost immediately called into question by a report by Peter Bergen, an al Qaeda expert, on CNN. The viewpoint summarizes the differing accounts and concludes that the most likely scenario is that there were three SEALs present at the climax of the raid, but the identity of the actual shooter responsible for the wound that killed Bin Laden may never be known. Rupert Cornwall is a writer and former Moscow correspondent for the British newspaper *The Independent*. He writes commentary on international relations and US politics and was

SOURCE. Rupert Cornwell, "Who Really Killed the al-Qa'ida Leader? SEAL Team 6 Member Disputes Interview with 'The Man Who Shot'," *The Independent*, March 27, 2013. Copyright © 2013 by The Independent. All rights reserved. Reproduced by permission.

previously a foreign correspondent for the *Financial Times* and Reuters.

The mission, like commando raids throughout history, depended on discretion and absolute secrecy. For those who took part, it was supposed to stay that way. Not a chance though, when this particular raid successfully took down the most wanted and most infamous man on the planet—and America's entertainment industry, money and politics entered the fray.

Thus it has been with the death of Osama bin Laden, ever since the US Navy SEALs' Team Six entered the nondescript compound in Abbottabad, Pakistan, in the early hours of 2 May 2011 and killed the al-Qa'ida leader, almost 10 years after he masterminded the bloodiest ever attack on US soil. Since then, time has brought not clarity but confusion, culminating in flatly contradictory accounts of precisely how bin Laden died, from the very SEALs who were supposed never to talk about it at all.

> The confusion began the very next day—and emanated from the very top of the chain of command.

Confusion Started Immediately

To be fair, the confusion began the very next day—and emanated from the very top of the chain of command, the White House itself. In their first version of how events unfolded, [President Barack] Obama administration officials claimed that the terrorist leader had perished in a bloody firefight, and moreover as something of a coward, using one of his wives as a human shield.

That account quickly changed in the light, it was said, of further debriefings of the commandos themselves. Bin Laden had not been armed at the moment he died, and the woman had rushed to protect him. But questions continued to be asked; this was after all one of the news stories of the decade.

Sixteen months later, in September 2012, they seemed to find an answer with publication of *No Easy Day* by a writer using the pseudonym Mark Owen—soon revealed to be Matt Bissonnette, one of the three SEALs who made it to the top-floor bedroom at the compound where bin Laden was hiding. The first of the three, the so-called "point man", had shot bin Laden, who lay fatally wounded on the floor. There Bissonnette finished him off.

The book, predictably, was a best-seller and stands to be the definitive (and, of course, highly lucrative) version of what happened. Unless, that is, you choose to believe a very different account, in the March [2013] issue of *Esquire* magazine and running to 15,000 words, entitled "The Man Who Killed Osama bin Laden".

It wasn't Bissonnette, said *Esquire*, but a man referred to simply as "the Shooter", now no longer in the military and very much down on his luck. "The man who shot and killed Osama bin Laden," the author, Phil Bronstein, began, "sat in a wicker chair in my back yard, wondering how he was going to feed his wife and kids, or pay for their medical care".

But he had a heroic tale to tell, how the point man had missed and that he, the Shooter, was the SEAL who burst into bin Laden's bedroom, where the al-Qa'ida leader had a gun "within reach", and killed him with two shots to the forehead. He then left the military—and unfortunately having not served the required 20 years, does not qualify either for a veteran's pension or his health coverage.

But in recent days the *Esquire* profile, too, has come under withering fire. First SOFREP, the news and blog commentary of the special forces, put out a piece unsubtly headlined "Esquire is Screwed: Duped by Fake UBL [bin Laden] Shooter", and added that the individual in question was now merrily cashing in on sympathy donations from the magazine's readers.

US soldiers and service members at Bagram Air Field watch news coverage of the Bin Laden assassination on May 2, 2011. The true identity of the SEAL who shot Bin Laden is not known as of 2014. (© Kristin M. Hall/AP Images.)

Then CNN, in the person of Peter Bergen, its terror analyst and long-time bin Laden expert, weighed in, interviewing an anonymous SEAL Team Six operator who told him that the Shooter "is talking complete B-S". This version, which closely resembles that of Bissonnette, is that the point man shot and gravely wounded bin Laden when he poked his head out of the bedroom door. The other two SEALs in the trio then entered the room and finished him off with two shots to the chest.

As for the Shooter, according to Bergen's source, he was kicked out of Red Squadron, the Team Six group that carried out the raid, for bragging about the mission in bars around Virginia Beach where the SEAL unit is based. For its part, *Esquire* is standing by its story, insisting that it is based on information from "numerous sources", including members of SEAL Team Six and the Shooter himself, as well as "detailed descriptions" of mission debriefs.

> Which of [the SEALs] actually killed Osama bin Laden may never be known.

The Truth May Never Be Known

There, for now, matters stand. What seems clear is that the three SEALs present at the climax of the Abbottabad operation were the point man, Bissonnette (aka Owen) and the unidentified Shooter. But which of them actually killed Osama bin Laden may never be known. The compound itself has been razed and, as always in such historical mysteries, the further from the actual event in question, the harder facts become to verify.

Bergen further quotes the SEAL team commander as his men personally briefed Barack Obama after the raid. "If you took one person out of the puzzle," the commander told the President, "we wouldn't have the competence to do the job we did. Everybody's vital. It's not about the guy who pulled the trigger, it's about what we did together."

> The SEALs have not lacked for credit and praise over the bin Laden operation.

But paeans to team spirit do not answer a separate question: how much should America's special forces commandos talk about what they do? Not at all, officials insist. But in *No Easy Day*, Bissonnette justifies the spilling of the beans, writing that it was "time to set the record straight", and that his book would "finally give credit to those who earned it".

Nonsense, say those in charge; whatever else, the SEALs have not lacked for credit and praise over the bin Laden operation. But this argument for anonymity hardly squares with the help given to the makers of *Zero Dark Thirty*—the movie of the hunting down of bin Laden—by the Pentagon and the CIA, who were only too anxious to share in the glory (if not the financial rewards) of the operation.

Last but not least, for Obama himself, 2 May 2011 was pure political gold—dispelling any lingering suspicion that this Democrat was "weak" on national security.

With considerations like these, discretion was always bound to be the first casualty of the killing of Osama bin Laden.

The Contradictory Accounts

White House version, 2–4 May 2011

According to the initial, White House version of Osama bin Laden's death, Navy SEALs shot the al-Qa'ida leader as he "engaged [them] in a firefight" and pulled one of his wives in front of him as a "human shield". But almost immediately administration officials backtracked, admitting bin Laden was unarmed when he was killed—although an AK-47 and a Makarov pistol lay within arms' reach, they claimed—and that his wife had rushed "the US assaulter and was shot in the leg but not killed". They blamed the divergent accounts on the time it took to process after-action reports from the SEALs. More controversy was to follow.

No Easy Day, 4 September 2012

Former SEAL Mark Bissonnette broke the commandos' code of silence last summer by co-authoring an account of the raid. Writing under the pseudonym "Mark Owen", he claimed bin Laden was shot in the head as he peered out of his bedroom door. Bissonnette writes the SEALs then found bin Laden crumpled in a pool of blood on the floor. At that point, Bissonnette claims he and his comrades trained their guns on bin Laden's still-twitching body, shooting him until he lay motionless. But US special operations chief, Admiral William McRaven, dismissed Bissonnette's account as inaccurate.

Esquire, 11 February 2013

Last month, *Esquire* profiled a pseudonymous SEAL who claimed he had fired the shots that killed bin Laden. In this version, "the Shooter" was right behind the "point man" as the two vaulted the stairs to the top floor of bin Laden's compound. As bin Laden poked his head out of his bedroom door, the "point man" shot, either missing or lightly wounding bin Laden, before peeling off to tackle two women in the hallway whom he believed were wearing suicide vests. "The Shooter" claims he ran alone into the bedroom where he found bin Laden standing behind one of his wives, with a gun within reach. He shot him twice in the forehead.

CNN, 26 March 2013

Now veteran Afghanistan reporter Peter Bergen claims that another Navy SEAL told him the account of "the Shooter" is "complete B-S". In this SEAL's version, the "point man" gravely wounded bin Laden, before gathering the two women who might have been suicide bombers in his arms to absorb the explosion. "Two more SEALs then entered bin Laden's bedroom and, seeing that al Qa'ida's leader was lying mortally wounded on the floor, finished him off with shots to the chest," Bergen writes—an account that closely matches the one in Mark Bissonnette's best-selling book.

Bin Laden's Death Brings Welcome Closure

David Paul Kuhn

In the following viewpoint, a journalist describes the mood across the United States after the announcement that Osama bin Laden was dead. He compares the expressions of patriotism and the bipartisan congratulations bestowed on the president to the unity felt by the country immediately after the September 11, 2001, attacks. He writes that it is important that American forces killed the man responsible for a number of taunting and devastating attacks on US interests. The author argues that the Bin Laden assassination makes the United States feel powerful once again. Although the news of the death also brings back terrible memories of 9/11, it also brings closure to those affected by the attacks, he says. David Paul Kuhn is the chief political correspondent for Real Clear Politics, a political news and polling data website, and the author of *The Neglected Voter: White Men and the Democratic Dilemma.*

SOURCE. David Paul Kuhn, "Osama Bin Laden's Death Brings Closure," RealClearPolitics, May 2, 2011. Copyright © 2011 by David Paul Kuhn. All rights reserved. Reproduced by permission.

There was a throng of Americans outside the White House late Sunday night [May 1, 2011], singing "The Star-Spangled Banner." One man held an American flag aloft with both hands. Dozens quickly grew to hundreds. It was shortly after the television networks went live with the news. Osama bin Laden is dead.

He was the mastermind of the most deadly attack on U.S. soil since Pearl Harbor [the attack on a US naval base in Hawaii by Japanese forces during World War II]. The hero of our enemy. The most powerful military in the world could not capture or kill this man. He was the singular face of al-Qaeda, of global jihadists, the bloody terrorist of the American mind, who receded but never fully left. He was the dark shadow that haunts victims who know no justice. The mass murderer seemed to have gotten away with it. All this war, so many dead, and we had not killed *him*. And then, suddenly, one random Sunday night, came the news. Bin Laden is *finally* dead.

There was Barack Obama taking the podium shortly before midnight in the White House. "Justice has been done," the president said in a brief national address. It was official. Hundreds of New Yorkers soon gathered at Ground Zero[1]. Some waved American flags. Fireworks were set off on one rooftop, across the river in Brooklyn. In Philadelphia, the attention of fans watching a close, well-played baseball game turned from the field of play to their handheld phones. The buzz among the crowd turned to a spontaneous chant: "USA! USA!"

America has known no antagonist like bin Laden since Adolf Hitler. The Saudi national [i.e., bin Laden] tried in 1993 to bring down the World Trade Center. He declared war on the United States and our allies and civilians. He directed the bombing of two U.S. embassies [in Dar es Salaam, Tanzania, and Nairobi, Kenya, in 1998], attacked—and nearly sank—a U.S. Navy ship of war [the USS *Cole*, in 2000], and then launched the great blow that killed nearly 3,000 people [i.e., 9/11]. He taunted America on video afterwards. Subsequent U.S. wars were relegated to the gray area between defeat and victory. No grand triumph to bookend that awful day. Then here it was, here it is, a national catharsis.

Killing bin Laden Has United Americans

Political unity has come with this momentous announcement, as it has before, if only fleetingly. Republican 2012 candidate Mitt Romney quickly came out with a statement at midnight congratulating the U.S. military *and* the president. Romney was not alone. Republican New York Rep. Peter King went on CNN near 1 AM and commended Obama for "doing the right thing" as the "guy who was on the line" if the mission failed. It echoed the accord felt after America's day of terror.

> It matters, in some psychic and intangible respect, that American forces did this deed. That we got the bastard!

It matters, in some psychic and intangible respect, that American forces did this deed. That we got the bastard! It's a moment to celebrate the Special Forces, the U.S. military, to feel American and proud and powerful. And how this nation yearns to feel powerful again. There's so much navel-gazing today over the supposed sunset of American power. If only for this moment, Americans feel triumph.

There will be repercussions as well. Pakistan will have to explain how bin Laden was less than 50 miles from Islamabad in a mansion, a compound, comfortable with family. American forces moved immediately to a heightened alert status to guard against any terrorist reprisals.

Could bin Laden's death also offer America the elusive end to its 9/11 wars? Americans overwhelmingly backed the Afghan war at its outset. But the majority have turned against this longest of American wars. Most of al-Qaeda left Afghanistan years ago. Perhaps Ameri-

can forces now can do so as well. Might this mean a more rapid withdrawal?

The War on Terror Continues

Yet we can also exaggerate this news. The nebulous war goes on. Fractured terrorist cells will not relent. You will still have to take your shoes off at airports.

The nation has experienced nothing like this moment since V-J Day [Japan's surrender in 1945 at the end of World War II]. But today's war is amorphous. It cannot realize a definite end. There will be no moment of surrender on a battleship. The threat remains. This is not World War II. America is not mobilized. Taxes were always raised to fund wars, but not the post-9/11 wars. Most Americans have no family in the fight. A small

Days after 9/11 and a few blocks from Ground Zero, a "Wanted Dead or Alive" poster for Osama bin Laden is displayed along with American flags on a statue in the Financial District of New York City. (© Timothy A. Clary/AFP/Getty Images.)

9/11

On September 11, 2001, 19 al-Qaeda-trained terrorists hijacked four U.S. commercial airliners. The hijackers crashed two of the jets into the World Trade Center towers in New York City and crashed the third jet into the Pentagon outside Washington, D.C. Passengers and crew battled the hijackers for control of the fourth jet, and it crashed into a field near Shanksville, Pennsylvania, short of reaching the hijackers' intended target in Washington, D.C.

The attacks caused the subsequent collapse of the World Trade Center twin towers, damaged the Pentagon, and killed approximately 3,000 people. Included in the death toll were hundreds of firefighters and rescue personnel who responded to the crashes at the World Trade Center site and who were in the process of rescuing those inside when the buildings collapsed.

Al-Qaeda (also known as al-Qaida), and its leader, Osama bin Laden (also spelled Usama Bin Ladin or Osama bin Ladin), subsequently claimed responsibility for the attacks. Al-Qaeda—operating out of Afghanistan under the protection of the fundamentalist Taliban regime—and allied Islamic extremist groups had publicly vowed a terrorist war against the U.S. and Western interests in an effort to establish pro-Islamist governments and fundamentalist Islamist social order throughout the world. Al-Qaeda also directed the 2000 attack on the USS *Cole* near the port of Aden, Yemen, and claimed responsibility for the bombings of U.S. embassies in Africa.

The September 11, 2001 attacks were the most deadly international terrorist attack in history and the largest attack on United States territory since the Japanese attack on Pearl Harbor on December 7, 1941.

SOURCE. *K. Lee Lerner, "September 11 Terrorist Attacks on the United States."* Encyclopedia of Espionage, Intelligence and Security, *vol. 3, K. Lee Lerner and Brenda Wilmoth Lerner, eds. Detroit: Gale, 2004, pp. 68–72.

military class in America does the fighting and dying, far away, on some distant land.

But bin Laden was also an intimate fury. He was the face of America's enemy. Americans will long remember where they were when they heard that he was killed.

It matters, politically, that President Obama brought the news. Obama noted how he authorized the attack. Presidents crave these commander-in-chief moments. It could have failed. Imagine the news of a bungled attempt on bin Laden. Domestic political opposition would have pounced on the president. [Former US president] Jimmy Carter's failed rescue of the Iranian hostages [Americans held in Tehran from 1979 to 1981] reminds us that presidents risk stature in these moments. Yet this will not somehow re-make Obama. He remains a president struggling to win back his mandate.

> Bin Laden's death will mean the most to those who lost loved ones [and] who survived the 9/11 attacks.

Welcome Closure for 9/11 Survivors

Ultimately, bin Laden's death will mean the most to those who lost loved ones, who lost a part of themselves, who survived the 9/11 attacks. Many of them had surely given up on ever knowing this emotion, this justice.

That tragic morning remains frozen in the American mind. The visceral chaos of the Twin Towers. Those of us who were there recall only scattered images. I remember the tide of humanity fleeing for their lives as the first tower collapsed. How the ground shook as the second tower fell. That choking dust and how it settled over downtown and gave beneath our feet when you walked on it by afternoon. How downtown New York became this apocalyptic, ashen world. And how little remained of the countless dead. Worlds smashed before us.

There were uplifting stories. A few early survivors. The ranks of relentless firefighters gathering on the West Side Highway by dawn. Men aching to return to the debris pile. But morale was low in those months after. Too many were dead. The fire had not gone out below. New Yorkers wondered if there would be another attack.

Bin Laden's death finds its way back to that malaise and grief. It returns us to the personal hells he wrought. Americans will recall it all, all over again. But, for the first time, those memories will carry a measure of closure.

Note

1. "Ground Zero" refers to the World Trade Center site in New York City, one of the US locations attacked by al Qaeda on September 11, 2001 ("9/11").

Osama bin Laden's Perverted Legacy

Harlan Ullman

In the following viewpoint, one of the chief architects of the military doctrine of "shock and awe" (the demonstration of overwhelming power to discourage an enemy) argues that al Qaeda has succeeded in weakening the United States in unexpected ways. He writes that al Qaeda's leadership, including Osama bin Laden, did not anticipate the consequences of the September 11, 2001, attacks. The subsequent refocusing of US military might on the war on terror has had increasingly negative effects on the United States, in his view. He argues that the financial expense alone is unsustainable. Moreover the assassination of Bin Laden promises to further strain the US-Pakistan relationship, he says. Harlan Ullman is a senior adviser at the Atlantic Council, an international political policy think tank, and an adviser to the North Atlantic Treaty Organization.

A bullet to the brain ended Osama bin Laden's life on Earth. But, in a perverse twist of fate, his death ironically and iconically strengthened a bloody legacy to the detriment of much of the civilized world in at least three powerful ways.

First, bin Laden abetted the economic and financial misfortunes of the United States through its extravagant pursuit of the global war on terror and in the process managed to set the U.S. military on a course in which its cost was too expensive to afford.

> "Bin Laden weakened the fundamental precepts of liberal democracies by catalyzing huge infringements on civil liberties."

Second, bin Laden weakened the fundamental precepts of liberal democracies by catalyzing huge infringements on civil liberties in the name of preventing future terror attacks.

Finally, by living and dying in Pakistan, bin Laden set in place a metastasizing cancer that could prove fatal to current U.S.-Pakistani relationships.

How could this happen? Answers begin on Sept. 11, 2001, and what surprised and shocked bin Laden and his colleagues after the attack. Al-Qaida had expected the remains of the Twin Towers to serve as smoking and enduring ruins to remind America of its weaknesses and vulnerabilities. Instead, the towers rapidly collapsed.

Nor did al-Qaida anticipate and even understand the huge economic and financial losses that would accrue to the markets that mounted in the trillions with disruption to banking, transportation and other business sectors that followed. Finally, bin Laden couldn't predict the American and Western response that drove him from Afghanistan after an extraordinarily short and cheap military-intelligence campaign or, more significantly, that the wars would continue for a decade.

Conflicts in Afghanistan, Pakistan and against global terror have cost the United States, so far, upward of

$1 trillion and possibly much more. That doesn't include the long-term costs of dealing with tens of thousands of veterans of those wars physically and psychologically wounded who need extended treatment and of course the expense of build downs and replacement of equipment. Defense has been one of the major contributors to the debt and deficits the United States is accumulating.

Fighting those wars has required wholesale refocusing of U.S. defense procurement and logistics that has been hideously expensive. Three striking examples drive this point home suggesting the real costs of what is called "asymmetric war." Improvised explosive devices, once known as "booby traps" have caused a majority of combat casualties. These devices cost pennies to manufacture. Yet, mine resistant vehicles to protect troops can cost $1.5 million apiece. We have tens of thousands of the latter.

> While U.S. military might is extraordinary in its capacity, the costs are simply not sustainable regardless of economic times.

Our troops today depend on bottled water and not the iodine pill in a canteen of suspect local water as their parents and grandparents did. The Pentagon reports that a gallon of bottled water transported to distant operating bases in Afghanistan runs about $800.

We depend on "unmanned aerial vehicles" known as drones to disrupt and destroy our enemies. Unmanned is oxymoronic. A total of nearly 200 people are required per drone, the majority of which analyze and collect data from locations inside the United States.

Clearly, personnel and procurement are the driving costs and reflect these trends. While U.S. military might is extraordinary in its capacity, the costs are simply not sustainable regardless of economic times.

The Patriot Act in the United States and camera surveillance systems for example in the United Kingdom impose on civil liberties. Airport searches and patdowns

An airline passenger goes through a full-body scanner at O'Hare International Airport in Chicago. Security measures enacted during the war on terror may reduce personal and civil liberties once taken for granted. (© Scott Olson/ Getty Images.)

are accepted even if of dubious constitutional standing let alone costs and questionable effectiveness. All of this is in the name of security and safety.

Bin Laden's final legacy was living and then dying in Pakistan. The shock, embarrassment and horror on the part of Pakistanis have had and will have profoundly negative impact on relations with the United States. The Pakistan army, long the only well-regarded institution in Pakistan, has likewise suffered being labeled incompetent or complicit. How this ends is tenuous at best and if not put on a solid footing will jeopardize any chance of a successful drawdown in Afghanistan.

Americans of course rejoiced in meting justice to bin Laden. Yet, few have even begun to think about dealing with his threatening legacy. Indeed, with the misnamed "Arab Spring" in disarray, the international situation is far more and not less volatile. Egypt, Libya, Yemen, the

Persian Gulf states and the Arab-Israeli-Palestinian conflict clearly are affected by these legacies and constraints on what the United States can or could do.

A cogent, clear-cut strategy is sorely needed. With pending elections in 2012 and ideological divides dominating political choices in Washington, there is no chance of this happening in either party. The United States will try to muddle through preferring band aids to necessary surgery or chemotherapy to cure the cancers that pervade the body politic.

Bin Laden is dead and that is a good thing. But who may have gotten the better end of the stick?

Bin Laden's Killing Raises Many Legal Issues

Thomas Darnstädt

In the following viewpoint, a German political expert argues that the assassination of Osama bin Laden may not be legal under international law and the laws of war. He explains that internationally recognized laws prescribe a process in which a criminal such as Bin Laden should be captured, put on trial, and punished. The author argues that the US administrations involved in the war on terror never sought true justice in the conflict with al Qaeda. He also calls into question whether the United States is engaged in a true war with al Qaeda. It is troubling, in his view, that the assassination took place in Pakistan and not within the geographic confines of the official armed conflict in Afghanistan. Thomas Darnstädt is a lawyer and a law and politics editor of the current affairs magazine *Der Spiegel*.

SOURCE. Thomas Darnstädt, "Justice, American Style: Was Bin Laden's Killing Legal?," *Der Spiegel*, May 3, 2011. Copyright © 2011 by Spiegel. All rights reserved. Reproduced by permission.

U S President Barack Obama gets precious few opportunities to announce a victory. So it's no wonder he chose grand words on Sunday night [May 1, 2011] as the TV crews' spotlights shone upon him and he informed the nation about the deadly strike against Osama bin Laden. "Justice has been done," he said.

It may be that this sentence comes back to haunt him in the years to come. What is just about killing a feared terrorist in his home in the middle of Pakistan? For the families of the victims of the 9/11 attacks, and for patriotic Americans who saw their grand nation challenged by a band of criminals, the answer might be simple. But international law experts, who have been grappling with the question of the legal status of the US-led war on terror for years, find Obama's pithy words on Sunday night more problematic.

> [The United States] never sought the kind of justice that would have seen bin Laden tried in an international court.

Claus Kress, an international law professor at the University of Cologne, argues that achieving retributive justice for crimes, difficult as that may be, is "not achieved through summary executions, but through a punishment that is meted out at the end of a trial." Kress says the normal way of handling a man who is sought globally for commissioning murder would be to arrest him, put him on trial and ultimately convict him. In the context of international law, military force can be used in the arrest of a suspect, and this may entail gun fire or situations of self-defense that, in the end, leave no other possibility than to kill a highly dangerous and highly suspicious person. These developments can also lead to tragic and inevitable escalations of the justice process.

It is unfortunate. And it is certainly no reason for the indescribable jubilation that broke out on Sunday night across America—and especially not for applause inside the CIA's operations center.

War Crimes and the International Criminal Court

After several attempts in the past, most notably in 1919 and 1937, the United Nations adopted the Rome Statute of the International Criminal Court [ICC] on July 17, 1998. The ICC is independent from the United Nations, and its relations with them is governed by an agreement that has been approved by the UN General Assembly. The treaty creating the ICC came into force on July 1, 2002, and by February 19, 2004, ninety-two states had become signatories to the treaty. The ICC's judges and prosecutor were elected in 2003. The court is based in the Hague [Netherlands].

In its founding statute, the ICC enumerates the crimes over which it has jurisdiction. These include genocide, war crimes, crimes against humanity, and crimes of aggression. The ICC accepts the 1948 Genocide Convention's definition of what constitutes the crime of genocide. The Rome Statute also provides a detailed definition of what constitutes a crime against humanity, which is markedly better developed than the definition provided in the Nuremberg Charter. It also defines several other essential terms, including extermination, enslavement, deportation and forcible transfer or torture. . . .

The Rome Statute affirms several

Not Everything the US Declares to Be War Really Is

But Obama and his predecessor [George W.] Bush never sought the kind of justice that would have seen bin Laden tried in an international court. As early as his election campaign in 2008, Obama swore he would "kill bin Laden" and finish the job begun by his predecessor after 9/11. "We went to war against al-Qaida to protect our citizens, our friends and our allies," the president explained on Sunday night. A US national security official didn't beat around the bush, telling Reuters, "This was a kill operation." And why shouldn't it be? The very goal of war is the defeat of the opponent, the killing of enemies through legal means. War is war.

In truth, it isn't quite that simple. And not everything that the United States declares to be war really is. Legal broadly accepted legal principles such as *nullum crimen sine lege* and *nulla poena sine lege* (there can be no prosecution, nor punishment, for acts that were not prohibited by law at the time). This establishes that, even though an act may today be defined as illegal, that law cannot be applied retroactively to a time when it was not yet a part of the legal code. The statute also affirms the concept of *non bis in idem*, which disallows double jeopardy: an individual cannot be tried twice for the same offense. In addition, it affirms the principle of individual responsibility, denies prosecutorial jurisdiction over persons less than 18 years of age, and establishes that there is no statute of limitation for the crimes under its jurisdiction. Finally, it expressly holds commanders and other superior officers responsible for acts carried out under their orders, and rejects the defense strategy of claiming immunity for individuals who hold (or held, at the time of the violation) head-of-state status.

SOURCE. *"War Crimes,"* Encyclopedia of Genocide and Crimes Against Humanity, *vol. 3, Jiri Toman and Dinah L. Shelton, eds. Detroit: Macmillan Reference USA, 2005, pp. 1144–1151.*

experts like Kress say it is "questionable whether the USA can still claim to be engaged in an armed conflict with al-Qaida."

It was certainly still war when Bush began the invasion of Afghanistan in 2001. Operation Enduring Freedom targeted the Taliban government in Kabul [Afghanistan] as well as Osama bin Laden's terrorist organization which it backed. At the time, al-Qaida maintained bases and training camps in Afghanistan—just like a warring party, in fact. The war on terror was understood to be an "asymmetrical war," and the laws of war also permit the targeted killing of non-state combatants, provided they are really combatants who are organized in units with a military-like character, and that they are integrated into those units either as armed fighters or as a leader who issues commands.

Was bin Laden Still Even Giving Orders?

For years, Osama bin Laden was, without a doubt, a combatant according to the latter definition. Many terror experts today, however, doubt that definition still applied to him in the end. "Al-Qaida has obviously had a network structure for some time. In a network, it isn't clear who gives the orders in individual instances," Kress says. "Outsiders also know very little about al-Qaida's structures in the Pakistani border areas. It is in no way certain that bin Laden still had the authority to issue commands as head of a quasi-military organization."

But if bin Laden was no longer a leader, it would no longer be permissible to treat him as an enemy combatant or kill him.

An armored vehicle and security barriers protect the entrance to the Jalalabad Air Field in 2007. Navy SEALs flew from this former airport in Afghanistan to Abbottabad, Pakistan, to carry out the Bin Laden raid in 2011. (© **NBC NewsWire via Getty Images**.)

Nor is it clear which conflict this operation was actually part of. The operation didn't take place on the actual battlefield of Operation Enduring Freedom, i.e. in Afghanistan, but rather on Pakistani territory. On this point, too, the official American view of international law also diverges from that of most experts on the subject. The commanders of the war on terror consider the entire world to be a battlefield. The US would seek to justify a military operation like the one that took place Sunday anywhere it believes the enemy is hiding—regardless whether it be in Europe or Islamabad [Pakistan].

Kress and the vast majority of other experts on the law of armed conflict find this view unacceptable. "The theater of an asymmetrical conflict is regularly confined to the territory of the country in, or from, which the non-governmental actors act in quasi-military ways," says Kress. "Anything else would lead to the incalculable escalation of the use of force." Or is another asymmetrical war raging on Pakistani territory today, with al-Qaida waging war against the government there? If so, what role does the Taliban play in this conflict? Or bin Laden, for his part?

> 'It is in no way clear that bin Laden, at the time of his killing, commanded an organization . . . conducting an armed conflict.'

"It is in no way clear that bin Laden, at the time of his killing, commanded an organization that was conducting an armed conflict either in or from Pakistan," Kress says.

What Business Did the US Have in Pakistan?

And what business did the United States even have acting within the territory of Pakistan, a foreign power? A military strike that crosses national borders, barring acts of self-defense, is generally viewed as an infringement on sovereignty—unless Pakistan's government requested help from the Americans.

Did Islamabad actually make that request? Obama sought to gloss over the subject on Sunday night. "Tonight, I called President [of Pakistan Asif Ali] Zardari, and my team has also spoken with their Pakistani counterparts. They agree that this is a good and historic day for both of our nations."

But was Sunday a good day for justice?

For years, the very principle of international law has been to pursue justice rather than war. On Sunday, Obama said that bin Laden's fate is a "testament to the greatness of our country." If the United States had used the same power it deployed during the invasion of Iraq to force tyrants such as [Iraqi dictator] Saddam Hussein or [Libyan ruler] Moammar Gadhafi—not to mention the mass murderer Osama bin Laden—into the dock of an international court, one might have believed him.

Bin Laden's Killing Was Lawful

Harold Hongju Koh

The following viewpoint was written in response to criticism that the killing of Osama bin Laden by US armed forces was not carried out in accordance with applicable laws. The author provides an extensive excerpt from his own speech delivered almost a year before the assassination. In the speech, the author lists the principles of law that inform US operations against al Qaeda. He further explains that individuals such as Bin Laden can be lawful targets under international law as belligerents. He states there was no question that Bin Laden continued to function in a leadership position in al Qaeda. Further he asserts that the operation against Bin Laden took pains to distinguish legitimate military objectives while avoiding incidental injury to civilians, and lethal force is permissible when an enemy belligerent does not surrender. At the time the viewpoint was written, Harold Hongju Koh was the legal adviser for the US Department of State. An expert in public and private international law, national

SOURCE. Harold Hongju Koh, "The Lawfulness of the US Operation Against Osama bin Laden," *Opinio Juris*, May 19, 2011. Copyright © 2011 by Harold Hongju Koh. All rights reserved. Reproduced by permission.

security law, and human rights, Koh is currently a professor of international law at Yale Law School.

I write in response to those who have raised questions regarding the lawfulness of the recent United States operation against Al Qaeda leader Osama bin Laden. United States officials have recounted the facts of that well-publicized incident, most recently in the interview of President [Barack] Obama on *CBS News 60 Minutes* on May 8, 2011. In conducting the bin Laden raid, the United States acted in full compliance with the legal principles previously set forth in a speech that I gave to the American Society of International Law on March 25, 2010, in which I confirmed that "[i]n . . . all of our operations involving the use of force, including those in the armed conflict with al-Qaeda, the Taliban and associated forces, the Obama Administration is committed by word and deed to conducting ourselves in accordance with all applicable law." The relevant excerpts of that speech are set forth below:

> 'The United States has the authority under international law, and the responsibility to its citizens, to use force, including lethal force.'

The United States agrees that it must conform its actions to all applicable law. As I have explained, as a matter of international law, the United States is in an armed conflict with al-Qaeda, as well as the Taliban and associated forces, in response to the horrific 9/11 attacks, and may use force consistent with its inherent right to self-defense under international law. As a matter of domestic law, Congress authorized the use of all necessary and appropriate force through the 2001 Authorization for Use of Military Force (AUMF). These domestic and international legal authorities continue to this day.

As recent events have shown, al-Qaeda has not

abandoned its intent to attack the United States, and indeed continues to attack us. Thus, in this ongoing armed conflict, the United States has the authority under international law, and the responsibility to its citizens, to use force, including lethal force, to defend itself, including by targeting persons such as high-level al-Qaeda leaders who are planning attacks. As you know, this is a conflict with an organized terrorist enemy that does not have conventional forces, but that plans and executes its attacks against us and our allies while hiding among civilian populations. That behavior simultaneously makes the application of international law more difficult and more critical for the protection of innocent civilians. Of course, whether a particular individual will be targeted in a particular location will depend upon considerations specific to each case, including those related to the imminence of the threat, the sovereignty of the other states involved, and the willingness and ability of those states

A video seized from Bin Laden's compound shows him watching himself on television, which may suggest that he was still connected to al Qaeda activities while hiding in Pakistan. (© Department of Defense/File/AP Images.)

to suppress the threat the target poses. In particular, this Administration has carefully reviewed the rules governing targeting operations to ensure that these operations are conducted consistently with law of war principles, including:

- First, the principle of *distinction*, which requires that attacks be limited to military objectives and that civilians or civilian objects shall not be the object of the attack; and

- Second, the principle of *proportionality*, which prohibits attacks that may be expected to cause incidental loss of civilian life, injury to civilians, damage to civilian objects, or a combination thereof, that would be excessive in relation to the concrete and direct military advantage anticipated.

In U.S. operations against al-Qaeda and its associated forces . . . great care is taken to adhere to these principles in both planning and execution, to ensure that only legitimate objectives are targeted and that collateral damage is kept to a minimum. . . .

> 'The use of lawful weapons systems . . . for precision targeting of specific high-level belligerent leaders . . . is not unlawful, and hence does not constitute "assassination."'

Some have suggested that the *very act of targeting* a particular leader of an enemy force in an armed conflict must violate the laws of war. But individuals who are part of such an armed group are belligerents and, therefore, lawful targets under international law. During World War II, for example, American aviators tracked and shot down the airplane carrying the architect of the Japanese attack on Pearl Harbor, who was also the leader of enemy forces in the Battle of Midway. This was a lawful operation then, and would be if conducted today. Indeed, targeting particular individuals serves to narrow the focus when force is employed and to avoid broader harm to civilians and civilian objects. . . .

[In addition] some have argued that the use of lethal force against specific individuals fails to provide adequate process and thus constitutes *unlawful extrajudicial killing*. But a state that is engaged in an armed conflict or in legitimate self-defense is not required to provide targets with legal process before the state may use lethal force. Our procedures and practices for identifying lawful targets are extremely robust, and advanced technologies have helped to make our targeting even more precise. In my experience, the principles of distinction and proportionality that the United States applies are not just recited at meetings. They are implemented rigorously throughout the planning and execution of lethal operations to ensure that such operations are conducted in accordance with all applicable law. . . .

Finally, some have argued that our targeting practices violate *domestic law*, in particular, the long-standing *domestic ban on assassinations*. But under domestic law, the use of lawful weapons systems—consistent with the applicable laws of war—for precision targeting of specific high-level belligerent leaders when acting in self-defense or during an armed conflict is not unlawful, and hence does not constitute "assassination."

> The United States acted lawfully in carrying out its mission against Osama bin Laden.

In sum, let me repeat: . . . this Administration is committed to ensuring that the targeting practices that I have described are lawful. (emphasis in original)

The Legality of Killing bin Laden Is Clear

Given bin Laden's unquestioned leadership position within al Qaeda and his clear continuing operational role, there can be no question that he was the leader of an enemy force and a legitimate target in our armed conflict with al Qaeda. In addition, bin Laden continued to pose an imminent threat to the United States that engaged our right to use force, a threat that materials seized during the raid have only further documented. Under these circumstances, there is no question that he presented a lawful target for the use of lethal force. By enacting the AUMF, Congress expressly authorized the President to use military force "against . . . *persons* [such as bin Laden, whom the President] determines planned, authorized, committed, or aided the terrorist attacks that occurred on September 11, 2001 . . . in order to prevent any future acts of international terrorism against the United States by such . . . persons" (emphasis added). Moreover, the manner in which the U.S. operation was conducted—taking great pains both to distinguish between legitimate military objectives and civilians and to avoid excessive incidental injury to the latter—followed the principles of distinction and proportionality described above, and was designed specifically to preserve those principles, even if it meant putting U.S. forces in harm's way. Finally, consistent with the laws of armed conflict and U.S. military doctrine, the U.S. forces were prepared to capture bin Laden if he had surrendered in a way that they could safely accept. The laws of armed conflict require acceptance of a genuine offer of surrender that is clearly communicated by the surrendering party and received by the opposing force, under circumstances where it is feasible for the opposing force to accept that offer of surrender. But where that is not the case, those laws authorize use of lethal force against an enemy belligerent, under the circumstances presented here.

In sum, the United States acted lawfully in carrying out its mission against Osama bin Laden.

The Fight Against Bin Laden Cost Much and Yielded Little

Tim Fernholz and Jim Tankersley

In the following viewpoint, the authors call Osama bin Laden the most expensive public enemy in US history. The authors claim that, by a conservative estimate, the fifteen-year hunt for Bin Laden cost the United States $3 trillion—an amount that has added to the national debt and even threatens to hobble the economy. While the conflict with al Qaeda is not historically the highest in human and financial costs, the authors argue that other conflicts have provided major benefits to the economy. The viewpoint specifically discusses how World War II, while extracting a heavy toll, also helped end the Great Depression and ushered in decades during which the United States was an undisputed economic power. The authors argue that the fight against Bin Laden has not stimulated the economy and instead led to destabilization around the world and to fulfilling

Bin Laden's vision of a bankrupt United States. Tim Fernholz is a reporter for *Quartz* and the founding editor of the magazine *Tomorrow*. Jim Tankersley is an economic policy reporter for the *Washington Post*.

T he most expensive public enemy in American history died Sunday from two bullets.

As we mark Osama bin Laden's death, what's striking is how much he cost our nation—and how little we've gained from our fight against him. By conservative estimates, bin Laden cost the United States at least $3 trillion over the past 15 years, counting the disruptions he wrought on the domestic economy, the wars and heightened security triggered by the terrorist attacks he engineered, and the direct efforts to hunt him down.

What do we have to show for that tab? Two wars that continue to occupy 150,000 troops and tie up a quarter of our defense budget; a bloated homeland-security apparatus that has at times pushed the bounds of civil liberty; soaring oil prices partially attributable to the global war on bin Laden's terrorist network; and a chunk of our mounting national debt, which threatens to hobble the economy unless lawmakers compromise on an unprecedented deficit-reduction deal.

All of that has not given us, at least not yet, anything close to the social or economic advancements produced by the battles against America's costliest past enemies. Defeating the Confederate army brought the end of slavery and a wave of standardization—in railroad gauges and shoe sizes, for example—that paved the way for a truly national economy. Vanquishing Adolf Hitler ended the Great Depression and ushered in a period of booming prosperity and hegemony. Even the

> 'We have spent a huge amount of money which has not had much effect on the strengthening of our military.'

massive military escalation that marked the Cold War standoff against Joseph Stalin and his Russian successors produced landmark technological breakthroughs that revolutionized the economy.

Perhaps the biggest economic silver lining from our bin Laden spending, if there is one, is the accelerated development of unmanned aircraft. That's our $3 trillion windfall, so far: Predator drones. "We have spent a huge amount of money which has not had much effect on the strengthening of our military, and has had a very weak impact on our economy," says Linda Bilmes, a lecturer at Harvard University's John F. Kennedy School of Government who coauthored a book on the costs of the Iraq and Afghanistan wars with Nobel Prize-winning economist Joseph Stiglitz.

Certainly, in the course of the fight against bin Laden, the United States escaped another truly catastrophic attack on our soil. Al-Qaida, though not destroyed, has been badly hobbled. "We proved that we value our security enough to incur some pretty substantial economic costs en route to protecting it," says Michael O'Hanlon, a national-security analyst at the Brookings Institution.

But that willingness may have given bin Laden exactly what he wanted. While the terrorist leader began his war against the United States believing it to be a "paper tiger" that would not fight, by 2004 he had already shifted his strategic aims, explicitly comparing the U.S. fight to the Afghan incursion that helped bankrupt the Soviet Union during the Cold War. "We are continuing this policy in bleeding America to the point of bankruptcy," bin Laden said in a taped statement. Only the smallest sign of al-Qaida would "make generals race there to cause America to suffer human, economic, and political losses without their achieving anything of note other than some benefits for their private corporations." Considering that we've spent one-fifth of a year's gross domestic product—more than the entire 2008 budget of the United States government—responding to his 2001 attacks, he may have been onto something.

The Cost Scorecard

A fleet of fighter jets and military personnel stand on the deck of the supercarrier USS *Carl Vinson*—the vessel used for Osama bin Laden's ritual burial at sea—in 2011. Each supercarrier in its class costs at least $4.5 billion to build. (© Cheryl Ravelo/ Reuters/Newscom.)

Other enemies throughout history have extracted higher gross costs, in blood and in treasure, from the United States. The Civil War and World War II produced higher casualties and consumed larger shares of our economic output. As an economic burden, the Civil War was America's worst cataclysm relative to the size of the economy. The nonpartisan Congressional Research Service estimates that the Union and Confederate armies combined to spend $80 million, in today's dollars, fighting each other. That number might seem low, but economic historians who study the war say the total financial cost was exponentially higher: more like $280 billion in to-

day's dollars when you factor in disruptions to trade and capital flows, along with the killing of 3 to 4 percent of the population. The war "cost about double the gross national product of the United States in 1860," says John Majewski, who chairs the history department at the University of California (Santa Barbara). "From that perspective, the war on terror isn't going to compare."

On the other hand, these earlier conflicts—for all their human cost—also furnished major benefits to the U.S. economy. After entering the Civil War as a loose collection of regional economies, America emerged with the foundation for truly national commerce; the first standardized railroad system sprouted from coast to coast, carrying goods across the union; and textile mills began migrating from the Northeast to the South in search of cheaper labor, including former slaves who had joined the workforce. The fighting itself sped up the mechanization of American agriculture: As farmers flocked to the battlefield, the workers left behind adopted new technologies to keep harvests rolling in with less labor.

World War II defense spending cost $4.4 trillion. At its peak, it sucked up nearly 40 percent of GDP, according to the Congressional Research Service. It was an unprecedented national mobilization, says Chris Hellman, a defense budget analyst at the National Priorities Project. One in 10 Americans—some 12 million people—donned a uniform during the war.

But the payoff was immense. The war machine that revved up to defeat Germany and Japan powered the U.S. out of the Great Depression and into an unparalleled stretch of postwar growth. Jet engines and nuclear power spread into everyday lives. A new global economic order—forged at Bretton Woods, N.H., by the Allies in the waning days of the war—opened a floodgate of benefits through international trade. Returning soldiers dramatically improved the nation's skills and education

> The wars we are fighting today were kick-started by a single man.

level, thanks to the GI Bill, and they produced a baby boom that would vastly expand the workforce.

U.S. military spending totaled nearly $19 trillion throughout the four-plus decades of Cold War that ensued, as the nation escalated an arms race with the Soviet Union. Such a huge infusion of cash for weapons research spilled over to revolutionize civilian life, yielding quantum leaps in supercomputing and satellite technology, not to mention the advent of the Internet.

The Costs of the War Against al-Qaeda

Unlike any of those conflicts, the wars we are fighting today were kick-started by a single man. While it is hard to imagine World War II without Hitler, that conflict pitted nations against each other. (Anyway, much of the cost to the United States came from the war in the Pacific.) And it's absurd to pin the Civil War, World War I, or the Cold War on any single individual. Bin Laden's mystique (and his place on the FBI's most-wanted list) made him—and the wars he drew us into—unique.

By any measure, bin Laden inflicted a steep toll on America. His 1998 bombing of U.S. embassies in Africa caused Washington to quadruple spending on diplomatic security worldwide the following year—and to expand it from $172 million to $2.2 billion over the next decade. The 2000 bombing of the USS *Cole* caused $250 million in damages.

Al-Qaida's assault against the United States on September 11, 2001, was the highest-priced disaster in U.S. history. Economists estimate that the combined attacks cost the economy $50 billion to $100 billion in lost activity and growth, or about 0.5 percent to 1 percent of GDP, and caused about $25 billion in property damage. The stock market plunged and was still down nearly 13 percentage points a year later, although it has more than made up the value since.

The greater expense we can attribute to bin Laden comes from policymakers' response to 9/11. The invasion of Afghanistan was clearly a reaction to al-Qaida's attacks. It is un-

> The greater expense we can attribute to bin Laden comes from policymakers' response to 9/11.

likely that the Bush administration would have invaded Iraq if 9/11 had not ushered in a debate about Islamic extremism and weapons of mass destruction. Those two wars grew into a comprehensive counterinsurgency campaign that cost $1.4 trillion in the past decade—and will cost hundreds of billions more. The government borrowed the money for those wars, adding hundreds of billions in interest charges to the U.S. debt.

Spending on Iraq and Afghanistan peaked at 4.8 percent of GDP in 2008, nowhere near the level of economic mobilization in some past conflicts but still more than the entire federal deficit that year. "It's a much more verdant, prosperous, peaceful world than it was 60 years ago," and nations spend proportionally far less on their militaries today, says S. Brock Blomberg, a professor at Claremont McKenna College in California who specializes in the economics of terrorism. "So as bad as bin Laden is, he's not nearly as bad as Hitler, Mussolini, [and] the rest of them."

Yet bin Laden produced a ripple effect. The Iraq and Afghanistan wars have created a world in which even non-war-related defense spending has grown by 50 percent since 2001. As the U.S. military adopted counterinsurgency doctrine to fight guerrilla wars, it also continued to increase its ability to fight conventional battles, boosting spending for weapons from national-missile defense and fighter jets to tanks and long-range bombers. Then there were large spending increases following the overhaul of America's intelligence agencies and homeland-security programs. Those transformations cost at least another $1 trillion, if not more, budget analysts say, though the exact cost is still unknown. Because much of that spending is classified or spread among agencies with multiple missions, a breakdown is nearly impossible.

The Hidden Costs of the Post-9/11 Wars

It's similarly difficult to assess the opportunity cost of the post-9/11 wars—the kinds of productive investments of fiscal and human resources that we might have made had we not been focused on combating terrorism through counterinsurgency. Blomberg says that the response to the attacks has essentially wiped out the "peace dividend" that the United States began to reap when the Cold War ended. After a decade of buying fewer guns and more butter, we suddenly ramped up our gun spending again, with borrowed money.

The price of the war-fighting and security responses to bin Laden account for more than 15 percent of the national debt incurred in the last decade—a debt that is changing the way our military leaders perceive risk. "Our national debt is our biggest national-security threat," Adm. Mike Mullen, chairman of the Joint Chiefs of Staff, told reporters last June.

> This war . . . has produced less—not more—stability around the world.

All of those costs, totaled together, reach at least $3 trillion. And that's just the cautious estimate. Stiglitz and Bilmes believe that the Iraq conflict alone cost that much. They peg the total economic costs of both wars at $4 trillion to $6 trillion, Bilmes says.

That includes fallout from the sharp increase in oil prices since 2003, which is largely attributable to growing demand from developing countries and current unrest in the Middle East but was also spurred in some part by the Iraq and Afghanistan conflicts. Bilmes and Stiglitz also count part of the 2008 financial crisis among the costs, theorizing that oil price hikes injected liquidity in global economies battling slowdowns in growth—and that helped push up housing prices and contributed to the bubble.

Most important, the fight against bin Laden has not produced the benefits that accompanied previous conflicts. The military escalation of the past 10 years did not stimulate the economy as the war effort did in the 1940s—with the exception of a few large defense contractors—in large part because today's operations spend far less on soldiers and far more on fuel. Meanwhile, our national-security spending no longer drives innovation. The experts who spoke with *National Journal* could name only a few advancements spawned by the fight against bin Laden, including Predator drones and improved backup systems to protect information technology from a terrorist attack or other disaster. "The spin-off effects of military technology were demonstrably more apparent in the '40s and '50s and '60s," says Gordon Adams, a national-security expert at American University.

Another reason that so little economic benefit has come from this war is that it has produced less—not more—stability around the world. Stable countries, with functioning markets governed by the rule of law, make better trading partners; it's easier to start a business, or tap national resources, or develop new products in times of tranquility than in times of strife. "If you can successfully pursue a military campaign and bring stability at the end of it, there is an economic benefit," says economic historian Joshua Goldstein of the University of Massachusetts. "If we stabilized Libya, that would have an economic benefit."

Even the psychological boost from bin Laden's death seems muted by historical standards. Imagine the emancipation of the slaves. Victory over the Axis powers gave

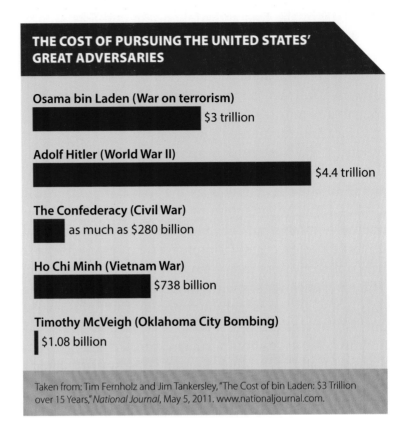

**THE COST OF PURSUING THE UNITED STATES'
GREAT ADVERSARIES**

Osama bin Laden (War on terrorism)
$3 trillion

Adolf Hitler (World War II)
$4.4 trillion

The Confederacy (Civil War)
as much as $280 billion

Ho Chi Minh (Vietnam War)
$738 billion

Timothy McVeigh (Oklahoma City Bombing)
$1.08 billion

Taken from: Tim Fernholz and Jim Tankersley, "The Cost of bin Laden: $3 Trillion over 15 Years," *National Journal*, May 5, 2011. www.nationaljournal.com.

Americans a sense of euphoria and limitless possibility. O'Hanlon says, "I take no great satisfaction in his death because I'm still amazed at the devastation and how high a burden he placed on us." It is "more like a relief than a joy that I feel." Majewski adds, "Even in a conflict like the Civil War or World War II, there's a sense of tragedy but of triumph, too. But the war on terror . . . it's hard to see what we get out of it, technologically or institutionally."

Bin Laden's Legacy in the United States

What we are left with, after bin Laden, is a lingering bill that was exacerbated by decisions made in a decade-long campaign against him. We borrowed money to finance the war on terrorism rather than diverting other national-security funding or raising taxes. We expanded combat operations to Iraq before stabilizing Afghanistan, which in turn led to the recent reescalation of the American commitment there. We tolerated an unsupervised national-security apparatus, allowing it to grow so inefficient that, as *The Washington Post* reported in a major investigation last year, 1,271 different government institutions are charged with counterterrorism missions (51 alone track terrorism financing), which produce some 50,000 intelligence reports each year, many of which are simply not read.

We have also shelled out billions of dollars in reconstruction funding and walking-around money for soldiers, with little idea of whether it has even helped foreigners, much less the United States; independent investigations suggest as much as $23 billion is unaccounted for in Iraq alone. "We can't account for where any of it goes—that's the great tragedy in all of this," Hellman says. "The Pentagon cannot now and has never passed an audit—and, to me, that's just criminal."

> More than actual security, we bought a sense of action in the face of what felt like an existential threat.

It's worth repeating that the actual cost of bin Laden's September 11 attacks was between $50 billion and $100 billion. That number could have been higher, says Adam Rose, coordinator for economics at the University of Southern California's National Center for Risk and Economic Analysis of Terrorism Events, but for the resilience of the U.S. economy and the quick response of policymakers to inject liquidity and stimulate consumer spending. But the cost could also have been much lower, he says, if consumers hadn't paid a fear premium—shying away from air travel and tourism in the aftermath of the attacks. "Ironically," he says, "we as Americans had more to do with the bottom-line outcome than the terrorist attack itself, on both the positive side and the negative side."

The same is true of the nation's decision, for so many reasons, to spend at least $3 trillion responding to bin Laden's attacks. More than actual security, we bought a sense of action in the face of what felt like an existential threat. We staved off another attack on domestic soil. Our debt load was creeping up already, thanks to the early waves stages of baby-boomer retirements, but we also hastened a fiscal mess that has begun, in time, to fulfill bin Laden's vision of a bankrupt America. If left unchecked, our current rate of deficit spending would add $9 trillion to the national debt over the next decade. That's three Osamas, right there.

Although bin Laden is buried in the sea, other Islamist extremists are already vying to take his place. In time, new enemies, foreign and domestic, will rise to challenge America. What they will cost us, far more than we realize, is our choice.

Mission Impossible: Bin Laden's Death Shows That the War on Terror Was Always a Fraud

Andrew J. Bacevich

The author of the following viewpoint argues that the war on terror is a fraud. He begins by stating that the assassination of Osama bin Laden is meaningless. In his view, the pursuit of Bin Laden was driven by the pursuit of power, not justice. As a result, the United States enlisted as its allies on the war on terror—in a cynical division of "with us" and "against us"—countries that were corrupt and authoritarian. The author explains how the policies of various countries in the Middle East have undermined US values and interests. In addition, he says, Pakistan has shown not to be a full partner to the United States despite military and other aid provided. The author says that restoring the purpose of the war on terror is impossible because the United States has been unable to recognize friend from foe. Andrew J. Bacevich is a professor of international relations and history at Boston University and has previously taught at the United States Military Academy at West Point and Johns Hopkins University.

The killing of Osama bin Laden settles nothing, decides nothing, and repairs nothing. Yet the passing of the al-Qaeda leader just might serve an important purpose. We confront a moment of revelation: coming across bin Laden comfortably ensconced in a purpose-built compound in the middle of major Pakistani city down the street from the nation's premier military academy should demolish once and for all any lingering illusions that Americans retain about their so-called global war on terror. The needle, it turns out, was not in the haystack but tucked safely away in our neighbour's purse—the very same neighbour who professed to be searching high and low to locate that very same needle. Think we've been had?

Bin Laden was an indubitably evil figure. Yet the historical drama in which he played a role of considerable importance is not a morality play. Its central theme is not good vs evil. It is instead the pursuit of power and advantage by whatever means are necessary. In short, the theme is politics—dirty, cutthroat, and no holds barred.

In the immediate wake of 9/11, President George W. Bush and more than a few other Americans insisted otherwise. The issue at hand, they asserted, could hardly have been clearer: it was freedom vs oppression; civilisation vs barbarism; tolerance vs bigotry; the law abiding vs the law defiling.

As in the early days of the Cold War, Washington divided the world into two neatly defined opposing camps.

'You are either with us,' Bush declared ten days after 9/11, 'or you are with the terrorists.'

The government of Pakistan, after brief hesitation and while under considerable duress, chose to be 'with us'. Overnight, it became a valued partner in the 'war on terror'. Pakistani interests and US interests now aligned, bonded together by the paramount importance of eliminating the threat to peace posed by al-Qa'eda. America's enemies were now Pakistan's enemies and vice versa—this at least was the prevailing assumption.

> Sustaining [a] happy picture of broad unity and lofty purpose required Washington to disregard any number of inconvenient facts.

Also 'with us' in this enterprise were Saudi Arabia and Egypt and Israel and many other countries, enlisted in President Bush's eyes in America's campaign to rid the world of evil.

Sustaining this happy picture of broad unity and lofty purpose required Washington to disregard any number of inconvenient facts. As it happened, Pakistan was known to have engaged in the illegal proliferation of nuclear weapons technology. Governed by a general who had seized power through a military coup, it was anything but democratic. Neither was Saudi Arabia, nation of origin for 15 of the 19 9/11 hijackers. Egypt was likewise an authoritarian state, its president blatantly rigging elections to keep himself and his corrupt cronies in power. As for Israel, its colonising of territories inhabited by Palestinians provided a motive (or pretext) that 'terrorists' skilfully exploited to provide a veneer of moral justification for their attacks against the West.

The lifespan of Bush's band of unlikely brothers united in a common pursuit of peace and freedom proved disappointingly short. The first defections came unexpectedly from 'old Europe', which opted out of the US plan to invade Iraq, Bush having failed to convince his French and German counterparts (with the Turks

following suit) that ousting a regime not involved in 9/11 and uncongenial to the religious radicalism to which Osama bin Laden subscribed held the key to destroying al-Qaʾeda. Indeed, prominent among the unintended consequences flowing from the overthrow of Saddam Hussein was the emergence in Iraq of an al-Qaʾeda affiliate where none had existed before.

Meanwhile, Saudi Arabia and Egypt were ignoring Washington's entreaties to embrace liberal reform, setting an example for others in the region. The logic of easing up on internal dissent and thereby opening the door to Islamic radicalism escaped them. For their part, successive Israeli governments—proclaiming their unswerving commitment to the 'peace process'—disregarded US requests to curb settlement activity. Instead, under the guise of erecting a defensive security barrier, the Jewish state embarked upon a de facto policy of partition and territorial annexation. Israel expected (and got) unstinting American support, but had no intention of compromising its security to further Washington's purposes.

The governments that the United States installed in Iraq and Afghanistan pursuant to occupying those two countries likewise proved less than fully compliant. To Washington's chagrin, post-Saddam Baghdad seemed eager to accommodate the Islamic Republic of Iran, senior surviving member of the infamous Axis of Evil. In Kabul, President Hamid Karzai grew tired of seeing his countrymen killed and maimed in allied friendly-fire incidents and talked of cutting deals with the Taleban, in clear violation of the American prohibition on negotiating with terrorists. Gratitude for all that the United States had done was in short supply.

Yet all of this was as nothing compared to the problems besetting US-Pakistani relations. During the decades prior to 9/11, Washington's relations with Islamabad had suffered many ups and downs, the United

Photo on previous pages: A US military Chinook helicopter delivers aid to Pakistanis affected by devastating floods in 2010. The United States provides humanitarian and military aid to Pakistan as a partner in the war on terror. (© Carl De Souza/AFP/Getty Images.)

States embracing Pakistan as an ally when it was convenient to do so and otherwise giving the country the back of its hand. Bluntly, neither members of the Pakistani elite nor the man in the street had any reason to trust Washington.

So despite constant cajoling and complaint, with generous US military and economic subsidies thrown in as sweeteners, Pakistani efforts to help snuff out violent Islamic radicalism have been, at best, half-hearted. Indeed, Pakistan is itself a state supporter of terrorism (directed against its arch-enemy India) and in all likelihood would like to see the Taleban restored to power in Afghanistan (again as a curb against Indian influence). Dissatisfied with Pakistani efforts to clean out Taleban sanctuaries inside its border, the United States has taken matters into its own hands, greatly expanding its campaign of aerial bombardment using missile-firing drones against targets within Pakistan itself. Unwilling to acknowledge that they allow US forces to disregard their country's sovereignty on a routine basis, senior Pakistani military and government officials make a pretence of professing shock and dismay, thereby encouraging Pakistani anti-Americanism to fester.

> Restoring even the appearance of purposefulness to the . . . war on terror has now become impossible.

Already enmeshed in crisis, the relationship between the United States and Pakistan now stands on the brink of complete collapse. Diplomats will attempt to paper over the differences, with one side offering lies that the other side may pretend to believe. Their efforts may even succeed in creating some semblance of normality. Yet it will be no more than a semblance.

Yet more important is this: restoring even the appearance of purposefulness to the enterprise once known as the global war on terror has now become impossible.

That war is a fraud. It exists only as a figment of American imagination. At great cost to itself and others, the United States has been playing the wrong game, falling prey to the tricks of its erstwhile friends, unable even to recognise who its enemies actually are.

Years After Bin Laden's Death, al Qaeda Remains a Threat

Graeme Green

The following viewpoint reports on the continuing threat posed by al Qaeda years after Osama bin Laden's assassination. The viewpoint states that the group has evolved since the start of the war on terror. The organization may be smaller in membership but not in influence, according to sources cited by the viewpoint. Although the group has become fragmented due to attacks by the United States and its allies, the smaller groups have continued to spread Bin Laden's ideology and tactics around a wide area of the Middle East, the author states. Extremism has actually increased because of military interventions by the West, according to the viewpoint. Graeme Green is an international journalist, travel writer, photographer, and editor based in London.

The death of Osama bin Laden was, for some, a full stop, America's revenge for the 9/11 attacks and the end of the al-Qaeda story.

But since bin Laden was assassinated in May 2011, the name of al-Qaeda—the group bin Laden founded—has continued to appear regularly in news stories around the world.

Recently, al-Qaeda has been connected to bomb attacks in Iraq, killings and conflicts in Mali, clashes in Yemen, and attacks and kidnappings in Afghanistan.

So, what state is al-Qaeda currently in? How has the organisation changed since the so-called 'war on terror' of the [US president George W.] Bush and [British prime minister Tony] Blair era? And do they still pose a significant threat?

'Al-Qaeda has declined in size but not in influence,' said Rohan Gunaratna, head of the International Centre for Political Violence and Terrorism Research.

'Although its numerical strength has depleted, its ability to shape and influence like-minded groups from Africa to the Middle East and Asia has increased.

'Today, in place of one al-Qaeda led by Osama bin Laden, there are 30 groups embracing al-Qaeda ideology and methodology.'

The structure of al-Qaeda has changed, says Raffaello Pantucci, senior research fellow at the Royal United Services Institute.

'Al-Qaeda is in a complex state. It's fragmented into a series of grouplets that all demonstrate some level of connectivity.

'However, they tend to be operating to primarily localised agendas. This is in contrast to the period around 9/11 when it was a much more coherent and structured

> 'Today, in place of one al-Qaeda led by Osama bin Laden, there are 30 groups embracing al-Qaeda ideology and methodology.'

entity with a core leadership and lots of units scattered around the world conducting different tasks.

'What is left of al-Qaeda core is based primarily in Pakistan's lawless provinces, with likely some overspill into Afghanistan and possibly Iran.

'Other groups with varying degrees of links to al-Qaeda's core can be found in the Sahel region—Mali, for the most part, parts of Libya too—and as far down as Nigeria.

'Over in Somalia, al-Shabaab, a group that pledged allegiance to al-Qaeda core over a year ago, is still operational, and across the water in Yemen, al-Qaeda in the Arabian Peninsula continues to pose a threat.

'The most active and bloody group is to be found in Iraq, where the Islamic State of Iraq (al-Qaeda in Iraq) is carrying out regular terrorist attacks and has links across the border in Syria.'

> 'Multiple affiliates across the globe have adopted al-Qaeda ideology and rhetoric [and] have given . . . bin Laden's vision a new lease on life.'

The fragmentation and dispersal is due, in part, to Western military action in al-Qaeda's original base regions, said Dr Rashmi Singh, a lecturer in terrorism studies at the University of St Andrews.

She said: 'Al-Qaeda has been in a state of fragmentation for considerable time. The trigger for this fragmentation was the US and allied attacks on Afghanistan and the dispersal of al-Qaeda core from the region into neighbouring Pakistan and beyond.

'This fragmentation has continued and even accelerated after bin Laden's targeted assassination.'

She added: 'However, we must remember that the core of bin Laden's vision for al-Qaeda as a movement was the spread of the al-Qaeda ideology of global jihad against both near and far enemies.

'In this, both the fragmentation and his own death have served to accelerate the spread of this ideology.

A security officer guards al Qaeda prisoners convicted of terror acts at a court in Sanaa, Yemen, in December 2013. (© Mohammed Huwais/AFP/Getty Images.)

'Multiple affiliates across the globe have adopted al-Qaeda ideology and rhetoric, harnessed these to their own regional aims and, as such, have given al-Qaeda and its ideology, as well as bin Laden's vision, a new lease on life.'

The continuing bomb attacks, conflicts, killings and kidnappings suggest that 'while al-Qaeda may not be capable of spectacular attacks such as 9/11 and Madrid in the West, they continue to pose a credible threat to security across the globe', according to Dr Singh.

Gregory Johnsen is a Yemen analyst and author of *The Last Refuge*. 'Yemen is a deeply divided country at the moment and al-Qaeda is attempting to take advantage of that by building up its infrastructure, attempting to recruit more fighters and planning future attacks,' he said.

'Al-Qaeda in the Arabian Peninsula (AQAP), the group based in Yemen, absolutely poses a threat to the West. This group has shown that it has both the capacity and the determination to carry out strikes against the US and UK from its hideouts in Yemen.'

There are worrying warning signs in African countries, too, including Somalia, says James Fergusson, journalist and author of *The World's Most Dangerous Place*.

'General Carter Ham of the Africa Command has warned more than once that al-Qaeda franchises across the continent could link up in terms of sharing arms and training,' he said.

'Whether this will really happen is still moot, but the threat of an al-Qaeda-inspired sub-Saharan insurgency, from Somalia in the east to Mali in the west, must be taken seriously.'

Mr Fergusson added: 'Al Qaeda has become adept at exploiting the world's ungoverned spaces, of which there are many in the modern world.

'When governments fail their populations—in terms of jobs, housing, security, the chance of a decent future—those populations are apt to look for alternatives, which, in many Islamic countries, may well mean Islamism.

'In the case of some young men, it may mean extremist ideologies like al-Qaeda's. Extremism is generally a symptom, not the cause, of social unrest. While governments in countries as diverse as Yemen, Somalia, Mali and Algeria continue to fail to provide their people with the basics of life, al-Qaeda is likely to thrive.'

US and British forces are also accused of exacerbating the problem with the invasion of Iraq and other military actions, including the continuing drone attacks that kill far more civilians than terrorist targets.

'There was neglect on the part of the West to counter the ideology of al-Qaeda and their associated groups,' suggests Prof Gunaratna.

'In response to the overwhelming lethal operational strategy adopted by the West, the threat of terrorism and its precursor, ideological extremism, has grown even greater.'

The world can expect to see more of the same in [the] future from al-Qaeda, said Dr Singh.

> 'Al-Qaeda will continue to sustain itself as both a core and affiliate organisation for some time to come.'

'Al-Qaeda will continue to sustain itself as both a core and affiliate organisation for some time to come,' she said.

'It seems increasingly that the core is no longer directing or closely involved with affiliate attacks and practices, something bin Laden aimed for.

'At the same time, given the number of militant groups willing to adopt al-Qaeda ideology and openly affiliate themselves with the group, while expanding their original agendas, it's more than evident the group will continue to survive, morph and pose a challenge for security forces around the world.'

CHAPTER 3

Personal Narratives

Bin Laden's Wives Describe the Raid

Abbottabad Commission Report

The following viewpoint is excerpted from a narrative by several of Osama bin Laden's wives. They spoke to a Pakistani government commission about the raid on their compound in Abbottabad that resulted in Bin Laden's death. The viewpoint retells their memory of the events of the night of May 1 to May 2, 2011. They explain hearing noises outside and then the sound of soldiers on their roof. Some of the wives and Bin Laden's children came face to face with US soldiers; a number of family members and others in the compound were killed or injured by the US forces. The survivors were taken away by Pakistani security forces, and the wounded received medical attention at a hospital. The Abbottabad Commission was established by a joint session of the Senate of Pakistan and National Assembly to investigate the US raid on the Bin Laden compound. Its final report, which was highly critical of the Pakistani government, was not publicly disseminated by the government and was published online by Al Jazeera.

SOURCE. "Chapter 2: The Fateful Night of May 1–2," *Abbottabad Commission Report*, Government of Pakistan, 2013, pp. 34–40.

Today was Amal's turn for the Shaikh to be with her. She was the youngest of his wives. Their rooms were on the top (or second) floor. The two elder wives, Khairiyya and Sharifa Siham had their rooms on the first floor. Like the rest of the rooms of the house they were cramped and small. But they had apparently sufficed for six years. After the evening meal and prayer Amal and the Shaikh retired for the night. Shortly past midnight, they were awakened by the noise of what at first sounded like a storm. Their three year old son, Hussain, was asleep in the room. They went to the balcony to see what was happening. But it was a moonless night and pitch dark. Amal reached to turn on the light but the Shaikh said "No!" He went to the door to call for his son, Khalid, who lived on the first floor with his mother Sharifa. Amal went to see her children. She had five children. When she returned the Shaikh's two daughters Maryam and Sumaiya had come up from their rooms on the first floor. They recited the Kalima (the declaration of faith) and verses from the Holy Quran. The Shaikh said American helicopters had arrived and they should all leave this room immediately. They were unwilling to do so. Maryam and her children went to the balcony. The Shaikh reached for his weapon.

> They heard noises that suggested . . . people may be on the roof.

At that moment they heard a blast outside the house. Simultaneously they heard noises that suggested to her people may be on the roof. They also heard persons coming up the stairs. Suddenly, Amal saw an American soldier on the landing outside the bedroom aiming his weapon at the Shaikh. She saw a red beam of light but heard no sound. She rushed the soldier and grappled with him in an attempt to take his weapon from him. But he screamed "No! No!" and shot her in the knee. She swooned and could not see anything. She could only hear

العربية

One of Bin Laden's widows is seen in their villa in Islamabad, Pakistan, where the wives were under house arrest in 2012. (© AY-Collection/SIPA/Newscom.)

the daughters of OBL [Osama bin Laden] being asked the name of the Shaikh. She recalled that while she lay injured on her bed the other ladies were taken downstairs. A considerable while later they heard a loud explosion which shattered the windows. Then there was silence. An hour or so later the Pakistan Army arrived and they were taken to hospital. That was how Osama bin Laden . . . met his end in Abbottabad around 0050 hours on May 2, 2011 according to his youngest wife, Amal Ahmad Abdul Fattah al-Saddah (Umm al-Ibrahim).

Sumayya, one of OBL's daughters, who reportedly also grappled with a US soldier, said she saw one of the helicopters land from her window and immediately rushed upstairs to her father's room. She was not sure whether the US soldiers entered the building from the roof or from downstairs. Everything happened very rapidly. Although she did not see her father fall, she saw him on the floor. He had been hit in the forehead and she knew he was dead. His face was "clear" and recognizable. According to her, blood flowed "backwards over his head." However, because of the dark she could not see very clearly. The American solders asked her to identify the body. She said "my father."

Her sister, Mariam, was asked the same question and she replied "Abdullah bin Muhammad." The soldiers did not understand her reference to the last part of her father's full name (which was Osama bin Mahummad bin Awad bin Laden). Sumayya then told Maryam "tell them the truth. They are not Pakistanis!" Finally, they told the Americans the body was that of their father, Osama bin Laden. They were then told to stand in a corner. When they were later led out of the room Sumayya looked back and saw her father's body was gone. According to her, it was less than ten minutes from the time they were first awoken by the noise of the helicopters and the killing of her father.

> Another American came into the room and told them they had killed Osama bin Laden.

Sharifa Siham said she was in her room on the second floor with her son, Khalid bin Laden, when they were awoken by the helicopters. Khalid went to the window and told his mother Americans had landed. He took his weapon and went upstairs to his father. After a change of clothes she went to see the children. Meanwhile, Khalid also came down to calm them. He then went upstairs again. Shortly afterwards, an American entered her room and took out the hard disc of a computer in the room. Then another American came into the room and told them they had killed Osama bin Laden.

The eldest of the wives, Khairiyyah, said she heard the helicopters and saw one landing from her window. She immediately rushed up to Amal's room. She heard the voice of American soldiers and saw them wearing masks walking in the courtyard. Khalid asked the ladies to move away from the window. He had his Kalashnikov and went out of the room. When she returned downstairs she heard American soldiers inside the house. They forced their way into her room. One of them appeared to be as frightened as she was. He "looked as if he had seen a witch!" He searched her roughly and at gun point took her to the room where the other ladies and children were huddled together. More American soldiers came and asked whether this was the residence of Osama bin Laden.

Khairiyyah said Khalid was moving between floors from his father's room upstairs and to the ground floor to check on the children of Abrar after hearing their screams. Shortly afterwards, Khairiyyah saw her daughters brought downstairs with their hands tied behind them. Sharifa then saw the body of her son, Khalid, lying on the stairs in a pool of blood. She knelt down to kiss his forehead.

> The ladies and children remained huddled together too frightened to venture outside the house.

When they were taken down to the ground floor they saw the bodies of Abrar and his wife Bushra. Their children were in the room unharmed. She was unsure whether her husband and son had been able to fire any of their weapons. The Americans had used silencers on their weapons. When they left, one of them spoke to them in Arabic with a Lebanese accent, saying they would return in 2 hours. The ladies and children remained huddled together too frightened to venture outside the house.

Maryam, the wife of Ibrahim, who lived in the annexe, said she went to bed at 10 PM on the night of the raid. Around midnight she and Ibrahim woke to a noise of a magnitude she had never heard before. Her daughter Rahma who was in the next room was extremely frightened. Ibrahim went to fetch her and tried to calm her and the other children. He then received a call on his cell phone and asked if it was his brother Abrar, who along with his wife lived on the ground floor of the main house. But there was no answer. Ibrahim shouted into his phone, "Abrar, I cannot hear you. I am coming." At that moment, there was a knock on the door and Ibrahim asked in a loud voice, "Is that you, Abrar?" He opened the door. From outside someone fired at him through the window. He seemed to duck to avoid the bullet. But he had been mortally hit and fell to the ground. As he fell his feet hit the door he had just opened and it closed.

Maryam felt a bullet graze her cheek and teeth, and she felt a bullet (the same bullet or another) hit her right shoulder. She fell. One of her younger children rushed to her crying "Mother, don't die. If you die what shall we do?" She heard American soldiers shouting at her to open the door. She told them, "You have killed my husband and now only my children and I are in the room." A soldier then shouted in Arabic, "If you do not open the door we shall blow the house up." Despite her injuries she managed to drag herself to the door and open it. The Arabic speaker looked American. He then went towards the main house. The other soldier spoke to her in Urdu and told her to sit next to the stairs outside the house.

Maryam said she heard the Americans land on the roof of the annexe. The roof was cemented so she heard the footsteps. She also heard the rattling of the staircase railing which were outside the annexe. Two American soldiers, according to her, were on the roof and another kept guard over her and the children outside the house. Another entered the house and carried out a detailed search of all the rooms including the godown. When the electricity returned at 003: hours, the Americans switched it off.

The Americans forcibly carried out a body search on Maryam and slapped her when she resisted. She cursed them saying "Allahu Akbar Alaeikum! (Literally, God is great against you!) The Americans were in the house for between 30 minutes to an hour from the time they killed Ibrahim.

At long last she heard vehicles entering the Compound and thought it might be the Pakistani police. She also saw other people walking around the annexe. One of them heard her son crying and called out to her in Pashto, "Sister, what has happened, and why is your child crying?" She replied, "Don't you know what has happened to us?" More people came to the window speaking Pashto assuring her that an ambulance was on the way. Then some officials entered the house. They asked her to collect some clothes to take to the hospital. Before leaving she went back to her room to kiss the forehead of her dead husband Ibrahim.

Maryam wanted to go to the main house to leave some of the children with Bushra. But she was not allowed to go there. She was told that Bushra was alright. She did not know Bushra had in fact been killed by the Americans.

> Wives, children and grandchildren were taken away from the Compound . . . [and] were able to take only a few possessions with them.

The wives, children and grandchildren of OBL, the children of Abrar, and the wife and children of Ibrahim survived. OBL, his son Khalid, his couriers i.e. the brothers Abrar and Ibrahim, and Abrar's wife Bushra were killed. After the initial questioning, the wounded wife of Ibrahim, Maryam, was taken to hospital. The rest were taken away for detailed interrogation by the ISI.

By the time the wives, children and grandchildren were taken away from the Compound by Pakistani security forces and Amal was taken to the hospital for her wounds to be treated, the Azaan for the Fajr prayer could be heard. They were able to take only a few possessions with them. Of their valuables they could find nothing except for two or three gold "biscuits" of ten tolas each. The Americans had taken away a jewel box with twenty gold biscuits and two gold lockets with emeralds. They also took a purse that contained the will of Osama bin Laden.

Khairiyyah had previously read the will but did not wish to divulge the details. She said it was not political and pertained only to personal and family related matters. Other reports suggested that the will said his children should not seek the leadership of Al-Qaeda.

An Abbottabad Resident Live-Tweets the Raid

Sohaib Athar and Jolie O'Dell

The following viewpoint consists of the live posts on Twitter by a man in Abbottabad during the raid on Osama bin Laden's compound. It begins with a Tweet that a helicopter was hovering above the town, annoying him. He shares that he believes that there may have been a crash of one or more helicopters; that people in the area think it might be a drone attack; that one person is believed dead and another injured. After connecting the events with the televised address by US president Barack Obama, he understands that he had been tweeting about Osama bin Laden's assassination. He then wonders what effect the events will have on life in what was a peaceful and quiet town. Sohaib Athar is a software consultant and coffee shop owner in Pakistan. Jolie O'Dell is a technology journalist who has reported on web development, web design, and mobile technology for Mashable.

Without knowing what he was doing, Sohaib Athar, a.k.a. @ReallyVirtual, has more or less just live-tweeted the raid in which terrorist Osama bin Laden was killed Sunday [May 1, 2011].

The IT consultant resides in Abbottabad, the town where bin Laden was found and killed by a U.S. military operation.

Athar first posted about events surrounding the raid 10 hours before the publication of this article, writing, "Helicopter hovering above Abbottabad at 1 AM (is a rare event)." He didn't realize that he'd been tweeting about a top-secret attempt to kill an internationally wanted terrorist until nine hours later.

> Athar speculates that he was two or three kilometers away from the shooting.

Athar reported that one of the copters he'd heard had crashed and that the aircraft were not Pakistani. We now know that four helicopters had been sent to raid bin Laden's mansion in the town, and one [crash landed at the compound].

During the raid, Athar speculates that he was two or three kilometers away from the shooting that took place. Once news broke that bin Laden had been killed in Abbottabad, Athar tweeted, "Uh oh, now I'm the guy who liveblogged the Osama raid without knowing it."

Athar further reported that traffic was shut down in some areas, and the army had cordoned off the helicopter crash site.

Yet, he remains humble. "I am JUST a tweeter, awake at the time of the crash. Not many twitter users in Abbottabad, these guys are more into Facebook. That's all."

Sohaib Athar @ReallyVirtual Tweetstream

Sohaib Athar

@reallyvirtual

Helicopter hovering above Abbottabad at 1AM (is a rare event).

12:58 A.M., 2 May 2011*

Sohaib Athar

@reallyvirtual

Go away helicopter—before I take out my giant swatter :-/

1:05 A.M., 2 May 2011

> I hope its not the start of something nasty :-S

Sohaib Athar

@reallyvirtual

A huge window shaking bang here in Abbottabad Cantt. I hope its not the start of something nasty :-S

1:09 A.M., 2 May 2011

Sohaib Athar

@reallyvirtual

@mochin all silent after the blast, but a friend heard it 6 km away too . . . the helicopter is gone too.

1:44 A.M., 2 May 2011

Sohaib Athar

@reallyvirtual

@mohcin the few people online at this time of the night are saying one of the copters was not Pakistani . . .

1:48 A.M., 2 May 2011

han3yy

@han3yy

OMG :S Bomb blasts in Abbottabad. I hope everyone is fine :(

3 Years Ago [2 May 2011]

Sohaib Athar

@reallyvirtual

@raihak Funny, moving to Abbottabad was part of the 'being safe' strategy

1:57 A.M., 2 May 2011

Sohaib Athar

@reallyvirtual

Since Taliban (probably) don't have helicopters, and since they're saying it was not "ours", so must be a complicated situation #abbottabad

2:02 A.M., 2 May 2011

Sohaib Athar

@reallyvirtual

The abbottabad helicopter/UFO was shot down near the Bilal Town area, and there's report of a flash. People saying it could be a drone.

2:10 A.M., 2 May 2011

Sohaib Athar

@reallyvirtual

@wqs figures, if they have the right to shoot planes flying over the president house, the must have the same instructions for PMA

2:14 A.M., 2 May 2011

Sohaib Athar

@reallyvirtual

@smedica people are saying it was not a technical fault and it was shot down. I heard it CIRCLE 3-4 times above, sounded purposeful.

2:15 A.M., 2 May 2011

Sohaib Athar

@reallyvirtual

@tahirakram very likely – but it was too noisy to be a spy craft, or, a very poor spy craft it was.

2:16 A.M., 2 May 2011

> 'I think the helicopter crash in Abbottabad, Pakistan and the President Obama breaking news address are connected.'

Sohaib Athar

@reallyvirtual

Here's the location of the Abbottabad crash according to some people>>> http://on.fb.me/khjf34

2:34 A.M., 2 May 2011

Sohaib Athar

@reallyvirtual

Two helicopters, one down, could actually be the training accident scenario they're saying it was>>http://bit.ly/ioGE6O

2:43 A.M., 2 May 2011

Terminalxpk X (TX)

@terminalxpk

A Major of the #Pakistan #Army's 19 FF, Platoon CO says incident at #Abbottabad where #helicopter crashed is accidental and not an "attack"

3 Years Ago [2 May 2011]

Terminalxpk X (TX)

@terminalxpk

The Major also says no "missiles" were fired and all such exaggerated reports are nothing but rumours #Pakistan

3 Years Ago [2 May 2011]

Sohaib Athar

@reallyvirtual

And now, a plane flying over Abbottabad . . .

3:39 A.M., 2 May 2011

Ibar Nazar

@Ibar_Nazar

1 dead and 1 injured in Abbottabad for heli crashed

3:57 A.M., 2 May 2011

Munzir Naqvi

@naqvi

I think the helicopter crash in Abbottabad, Pakistan and the President Obama breaking news address are connected.

10:45 P.M., 1 May 2011 [7:45 A.M., 2 May 2011, Pakistan time]

Sohaib Athar

@reallyvirtual

Report from a taxi driver: The army has cordoned off the crash area and is conducting door-to-door search in the surrounding

> Uh oh, there goes the neighborhood :-/

8:02 A.M., 2 May 2011

Sohaib Athar

@reallyvirtual

Report from a sweeper: A family also died in the crash, and one of the helicopter riders got away and is now being searched for.

8:21 A.M., 2 May 2011

Sohaib Athar

@reallyvirtual

@kursed Well, there were at least two copters last night, I heard one but a friend heard two, for 15-20 minutes.

8:24 A.M., 2 May 2011

Sohaib Athar

@reallyvirtual

@kursed I think I should take out my big blower to blow the fog of war away and see the clearer picture.

8:24 A.M., 2 May 2011

Sohaib Athar

@reallyvirtual

I guess Abbottabad is going to get as crowded as the

Lahore that I left behind for some peace and quiet. *sigh*

8:27 A.M., 2 May 2011

Sohaib Athar

@reallyvirtual

RT @ISuckBigTime: osama Bin Laden killed in Abbottabad, Pakistan.: ISI has confirmed it << Uh oh, there goes the neighborhood :-/

8:31 A.M., 2 May 2011

Note

* When this viewpoint was originally published, the time stamp on each Tweet showed US Eastern time. All dates and times have been changed to reflect local Pakistan time.

President Obama Nervously Watches the Raid

Barack Obama, interviewed by Steve Kroft

In the following viewpoint, US president Barack Obama and a journalist discuss the assassination of Osama bin Laden a few days after the raid. He explains that catching Bin Laden was a priority for his administration, and the CIA continued its search for the al Qaeda leader's whereabouts with the new chief that the president installed at the agency. In his telling, unprecedented cooperation between the military and the CIA resulted in the successful completion of the plan to eliminate Bin Laden. The president also says that he is aware that every military decision he makes as commander in chief may result in casualties, and care is taken to avoid deaths among civilians and military personnel. He also reiterates his belief that justice was done by killing Bin Laden. Obama is the forty-fourth president of the United States. Steve Kroft is an investigative journalist and a longtime correspondent for *60 Minutes*.

SOURCE. Barack Obama, "Obama on bin Laden: The Full *60 Minutes* Interview," CBS News, May 15, 2011. Copyright © 2011 by CBS News. All rights reserved. Reproduced by permission.

Steve Kroft: When the CIA first brought [evidence of bin Laden's whereabouts] to you . . . what was your reaction? Was there a sense of excitement? Did this look promising from the very beginning? . . .

President Barack Obama: Shortly after I got into office, I brought [CIA director] Leon Panetta privately into the Oval Office and I said to him, "We need to redouble our efforts in hunting bin Laden down. And I want us to start putting more resources, more focus, and more urgency into that mission."

Leon took that to the CIA. They had been working steadily on this since 2001, obviously. And there were a range of threads that were out there that hadn't quite been pulled all together. They did an incredible job during the course of a year and a half to pull on a number of these threads until we were able to identify a courier who was known to be a bin Laden associate, to be able to track them to this compound.

> 'If in fact . . . we've got a good chance that we've got [Bin Laden], how are we gonna deal with him?'

So by the time they came to me they had worked up an image of the compound, where it was and the factors that led them to conclude that this was the best evidence that we had regarding bin Laden's whereabouts since Tora Bora.

But we didn't have a photograph of bin Laden in that building. There was no direct evidence of his presence. And so the CIA continued to build the case meticulously over the course of several months. What I told them when they first came to me with this evidence was: "Even as you guys are building a stronger intelligence case, let's also start building an action plan to figure out if in fact we make a decision that this is him or we've got a good chance that we've got him, how are we gonna deal with him? How can we get at that?"

And so at that point you probably had unprecedented cooperation between the CIA and our military in starting to shape an action plan that ultimately resulted in success this week.

Setting the Plan in Motion

When was that when you set that plan in motion?

Well, they first came to me in August of last year [2010] with evidence of the compound. And they said that they had more work to do on it, but at that point they had enough that they felt that it was appropriate for us to start doing some planning. And so from that point on we started looking at the time what our options might be.

The vigorous planning did not begin until early this year. And obviously over the last two months it's been very intensive in which not only did an action plan get developed, but our guys actually started practicing being able to execute.

> We had multiple meetings in the Situation Room in which we . . . would actually have a model of the compound and discuss how this operation might proceed.

How actively were you involved in that process?

About as active as any project that I've been involved with since I've been President.

Obviously we have extraordinary guys. Our Special Forces are the best of the best. And so I was not involved in designing the initial plan. But each iteration of that plan they'd bring back to me. Make a full presentation. We would ask questions.

We had multiple meetings in the Situation Room in which we would map out—and we would actually have a model of the compound and discuss how this operation might proceed, and what various options there were because there was more than one way in which we might go about this.

And in some ways sending in choppers and actually puttin' our guys on the ground entailed some greater risks than some other options. I thought it was important, though, for us to be able to say that we'd definitely got the guy. We thought that it was important for us to be able to exploit potential information that was on the ground in the compound if it did turn out to be him.

We thought that it was important for us not only to protect the lives of our guys, but also to try to minimize collateral damage in the region because this was in a residential neighborhood. I mean one of the ironies of this is, you know, I think the image that bin Laden had tried to promote was that he was an ascetic, living in a cave. This guy was living in a million dollar compound in a residential neighborhood.

Were you surprised when they came to you with this compound right in the middle of sort of the military center of Pakistan?

Well, I think that there had been discussions that this guy might be hiding in plain sight. And we knew that some al Qaeda operatives, high level targets basically, just blended into the crowd like this.

I think we were surprised when we learned that this compound had been there for five or six years, and that it was in an area in which you would think that potentially he would attract some attention. So yes, the answer is that we were surprised that he could maintain a compound like that for that long without there being a tip off. . . .

A Difficult Decision

What was the most difficult part? I mean you had to decide. This was your decision—whether to proceed or not and how to proceed. What was the most difficult part of that decision?

> The most difficult part is always the fact that you're sending guys into harm's way.

The most difficult part is always the fact that you're sending guys into harm's way. And there are a lot of things that could go wrong. I mean there're a lot of moving parts here. So my biggest concern was, if I'm sending those guys in and Murphy's Law applies and somethin' happens, can we still get our guys out? So that's point number one.

Point number two, these guys are goin' in in, you know, the darkest of night. And they don't know what they're gonna find there. They don't know if the building is rigged. They don't know if, you know, there are explosives that are triggered by a particular door opening. So huge risks that these guys are taking.

And so my number one concern was: if I send them in, can I get them out? And a lot of the discussion we had during the course of planning was how do we make sure there's backup? How do we make sure that there's redundancy built into the plan so that we have the best chance of getting our guys out? That's point number one.

Point number two was: as outstanding a job as our intelligence teams did—and I cannot praise them enough, they did an extraordinary job with just the slenderest of bits of information to piece this all together—at the end of the day, this was still a 55/45 situation. I mean, we could not say definitively that bin Laden was there. Had he not been there, then there would have been significant consequences.

Obviously, we're going into the sovereign territory of another country and landing helicopters and conducting a military operation. And so if it turns out that it's a wealthy, you know, prince from Dubai who's in this compound, and, you know, we've sent Special Forces in—we've got problems. So there were risks involved geopolitically in making the decision.

But my number one concern was: can our guys get in and get out safely. The fact that our Special Forces have become so good—these guys perform at levels that 20, 30 years ago would not have happened—I think finally gave me the confidence to say, "Let's go ahead." I think that the American people have some sense of how good these guys are, but until you actually see 'em and meet them, it's hard to describe how courageous, how tough, how skilled, how precise they are. And it was because of their skills that I ended up having confidence to make the decision. . . .

How much did some of the past failures, like the Iran hostage rescue attempt, how did that weigh on you? I mean . . .

I thought about that.

. . . was that a factor?

Absolutely. Absolutely. No, I mean you think about Black Hawk Down. You think about what happened with the Iranian rescue. And it, you know, I am very sympathetic to the situation for other Presidents where you make a decision, you're making your best call, your best shot, and something goes wrong—because these are tough, complicated operations. And yeah, absolutely. The day before I was thinkin' about this quite a bit.

It sounds like you made a decision that you could accept failure. You didn't want failure but after looking at . . .

Yeah.

. . . the 55/45 thing that you mentioned, you must have at some point concluded that the advantages outweighed the risks . . .

I concluded that it was worth it. And the reason that I concluded it was worth it was that we have devoted enormous blood and treasure in fighting back against al Qaeda. Ever since 2001. And even before with the embassy bombing in Kenya. . . .

> It was worth it [because] we have devoted enormous blood and treasure in fighting back against al Qaeda.

The Mood in the Situation Room

I want to go [in our discussion] to the Situation Room. What was the mood?

Tense.

People talking?

Yeah, but doing a lot of listening as well, 'cause we were able to monitor the situation in real time. Getting reports back from Bill McRaven, the head of our special forces operations, as well as Leon Panetta. And you know, there were big chunks of time in which all we were doin' was just waiting. And it was the longest 40 minutes of my life with the possible exception of when Sasha got meningitis when she was three months old, and I was waiting for the doctor to tell me that she was all right. It was a very tense situation.

Were you nervous?

Yes.

What could you see?

As I said, we were monitoring the situation. And we knew as events unfolded what was happening in and around the compound, but we could not get information clearly about what was happening inside the compound.

Right. And that went on for a long time? Could you hear gunfire?

We had a sense of when gunfire and explosions took place.

Flashes?

Yeah. And we also knew when one of the helicopters went down in a way that wasn't according to plan. And, as you might imagine, that made us more tense.

So it got off to a bad start?

Well, it did not go exactly according to plan, but this is exactly where all the work that had been done anticipating what might go wrong made a huge difference.

There was a backup plan?

There was a backup plan.

You had to blow up some walls?

We had to blow up some walls.

When was the first indication you got that you had found the right place? That bin Laden was in there?

There was a point before folks had left, before we had gotten everybody back on the helicopter and were flying back to base, where they said Geronimo has been killed. And Geronimo was the code name for bin Laden. And now obviously at that point these guys were operating in the dark with all kinds of stuff going on so everybody was cautious. But at that point cautiously optimistic.

What was your reaction when you heard those words?

I was relieved and I wanted to make sure those guys got over the Pakistan border and landed safely. And I think deeply proud and deeply satisfied of my team.

> I was relieved. . . . And I think deeply proud and deeply satisfied of my team.

Identifying bin Laden
When did you start to feel comfortable that bin Laden had been killed?

When they landed we had very strong confirmation at that point that it was him. Photographs had been taken. Facial analysis indicated that in fact it was him. We hadn't yet done DNA testing, but at that point we were 95 percent sure.

Did you see the pictures?

Yes.

What was your reaction when you saw them?

It was him. . . .

Was it your decision to bury him at sea?

It was a joint decision. We thought it was important to think through ahead of time how we would dispose of the body if he were killed in the compound. And I think that what we tried to do was, consulting with experts in Islamic law and ritual, to find something that was appropriate that was respectful of the body.

Frankly we took more care on this than, obviously, bin Laden took when he killed 3,000 people. He didn't have much regard for how they were treated and desecrated. But that, again, is somethin' that makes us different. And I think we handled it appropriately.

When the mission was over . . .

Uh-huh.

. . . and you walked out of the situation room . . .

Yeah.

. . . what did you do? What was the first thing you did?

Yeah, I think I walked up with my team, and I just said, "We got him." And I expressed my profound gratitude and pride to the team that had worked on this.

I mean keep in mind this is something, first of all, that that wasn't just our doing. Obviously since 2001, countless folks in our intelligence community and our military had worked on this issue. President [George W.] Bush had obviously devoted a lot of resources to this, and so there was a cumulative effort and a testament to the capacity of the United States of America to follow through. And to do what we said we're gonna do. Even across administrations, across party lines and the skill with which our intelligence and military folks operated in this was indescribable.

So it was a moment of great pride for me to see our capacity as a nation to execute something this difficult this well. And obviously, it also made me think about those families that I had met previously who had been so profoundly burdened by the fact that he was still runnin' around out there.

You know, I got a letter the day after, an e-mail from a young person who had spoken to her dad when she was four years old before the towers collapsed, he was in the building. And she described what it had been like for the last ten years growing up, always having that image of her father's—the sound of her father's voice, and thinking that she'd never see him again, and watching her mother weep on the phone. And that's what I thought about.

The US Relationship with Pakistan

When you announced that bin Laden had been killed last Sunday, you said "Our counterterrorism cooperation with Pakistan helped lead us to bin Laden in the compound where he was hiding." Can you be more specific on that, and how much help did Pakistan actually provide in getting rid of bin Laden.

You know, I've gotta be careful about sources and methods and how we operate and how we pieced together this intelligence, because we're gonna still be goin' after terrorists in the future.

What I can say is that Pakistan, since 9/11, has been a strong counterterrorism partner with us. There have been times where we've had disagreements. There have been times where we wanted to push harder, and for various concerns, they might have hesitated. And those differences are real. And they'll continue.

But the fact of the matter is, is that we've been able to kill more terrorists on Pakistani soil than just about any place else. We could not have done that without Pakistani cooperation. And I think that this will be an important moment in which Pakistan and the United States gets together and says, "All right, we've gotten bin Laden, but we've got more work to do. And are there ways for us to

> I didn't tell most people here in the White House. . . . It was that important for us to maintain operational security.

work more effectively together than we have in the past?"

And that's gonna be important for our national security. It doesn't mean that there aren't gonna be times where we're gonna be frustrated with Pakistanis. And frankly, there are gonna be times where they're frustrated with us. You know, they've got not only individual terrorists there, but there's also a climate inside of Pakistan that sometimes is deeply anti-American. And it makes it more difficult for us to be able to operate there effectively.

But I do think that it's important for the American people to understand that we've got a stake in continuing cooperation from Pakistan on these issues.

You didn't tell anybody in the Pakistani government or the military?

No.

Or their intelligence community?

No.

Because you didn't trust?

As I said, I didn't tell most people here in the White House. I didn't tell my own family. It was that important for us to maintain operational security.

But you were carrying out this operation in Pakistan.

Yeah.

You didn't trust 'em?

If I'm not revealing to some of my closest aides what we're doin', then I sure as heck am not gonna be revealing it to folks who I don't know.

Right. Now the location of this house, the location of the compound just raises all sorts of questions.

Uh-huh.

Do you believe people in the Pakistani government, Pakistani intelligence agencies knew that bin Laden was living there?

We think that there had to be some sort of support network for bin Laden inside of Pakistan. But we don't know who or what that support network was. We don't know whether there might have been some people inside of government, people outside of government, and that's something that we have to investigate, and more importantly, the Pakistani government has to investigate.

And we've already communicated to them, and they have indicated they have a profound interest in finding out what kinds of support networks bin Laden might have had. But these are questions that we're not gonna be able to answer three or four days after the event. It's gonna take some time for us to be able to exploit the intelligence that we were able to gather on site.

And I just want the American people to think about this. These guys, our guys, go in in the dead of night, it's pitch black, they're takin' out walls, false doors, gettin' shot at, they killed bin Laden, and they had the presence of mind to still gather up a whole bunch of bin Laden's material which will be a treasure trove of information that could serve us very well in the weeks and months to come. It's just an indication of the extraordinary work that they did.

The Bin Laden Situation Room Revisited— One Year Later

Jamie Crawford

Senior White House and national security staff congregated in the White House's situation room to watch the raid on the Bin Laden compound the night of May 1 to May 2, 2011. A photo of the meeting was widely disseminated after the president announced that Osama bin Laden had been killed. The following viewpoint is a summary, compiled one year after the raid, of the personal thoughts of the people in the photograph about the events of the day and night of the raid. Jamie Crawford is a CNN national security producer.

In the annals of American history, the famous photo taken by Pete Souza of President Barack Obama and his national security team monitoring Operation Neptune's Spear—the Navy SEALs raid that killed Osama bin Laden—has achieved icon status. Splashed across newspapers and television screens across the world, the tension in the room seemed palpable to all who saw it. But an interesting footnote to the famous photo is that it was not taken in the actual Situation Room at the White House.

As CNN Terrorism Analyst Peter Bergen reports in his new book *Manhunt*, about the decade long search for bin Laden, the room where the photo was taken is actually a smaller room adjoined to the larger Situation Room. Like the Situation Room, the smaller room has secure video and phone communications, but it has a table that can only accommodate seven people Bergen

Barack Obama, Joe Biden, Hillary Clinton, and members of the national security team react to a live update on the mission against Osama bin Laden as it is happening on May 1, 2011. (© Pete Souza/The White House via Getty Images.)

writes, as opposed to the larger table next door which can seat more than a dozen.

Brigadier General Marshall "Brad" Webb, assistant commanding general of Joint Special Operations Command who sits in the center of the famous photo, was monitoring the operation on a screen through a laptop computer. Michael Leiter, then director of the National Counterterrorism Center, went into the room to watch the feed that was being relayed from a secret drone. Secretaries [Hillary] Clinton, [Robert] Gates, and Vice President [Joe] Biden soon followed. Moments later Bergen reports, the president walked in and said, "I need to watch this," as he seated himself next to Webb.

In the days and months that followed, many of the people in the room have reflected on that crucial time in U.S. history, what it meant to them, and what they were thinking.

President Barack Obama

In a recent interview with NBC News, Obama said he thinks the photo was taken at about the time the helicopter went down.

In the days after the raid, Obama told CBS's *60 Minutes* that the raid was "the longest 40 minutes" of his life with the possible exception of when his younger daughter Sasha became sick with meningitis when she was three months old.

When they received word the helicopters carrying the Navy SEALs and the bin Laden body had left Pakistani airspace, the first person Obama called was his immediate predecessor, former President George W. Bush, to inform him of the operation. Obama also called former President Bill Clinton that evening as well.

Vice President Joe Biden

Vice President Joe Biden was opposed to going forward with the raid all the way up to the point when Obama made the decision to proceed. In remarks to House Democrats at their annual retreat earlier this year, Biden recalled the final moments before the commander-in-chief made his decision. Obama went around the table of his senior national security team to get their thoughts on whether the operation should go forward.

> 'I thought, "Man, that is a gutsy call."'

"He got to me. He said Joe, what do you think?" Biden recalled. "I said, we owe the man a direct answer. Mr. President, my suggestion is, don't go. We have to do two more things to see if he's there."

Biden told an audience in New York last week that Obama's decision to ultimately go ahead with the decision shows the president has a "backbone like a ramrod."

Anthony Blinken, National Security Adviser to Vice President Biden

On the morning of April 29, President Obama gathered with Tom Donilon, his national security adviser, White House Chief of Staff William Daley, Deputy National Security Advisor Denis McDonough, and his counter-terrorism adviser, John Brennan, and told the men he had made the decision to go forward with the operation. Anthony Blinken, Biden's national security adviser, heard the news shortly thereafter.

In an interview with Bergen, Blinken was somewhat surprised of the decision.

"I thought, 'Man, that is a gutsy call,'" Blinken told Bergen. "First, we don't know for sure bin Laden is there; the evidence is circumstantial. Second, most of his senior advisors recommended a different course of action."

Obama's presidency and the lessons of history also hung in the balance Blinken thought.

"Leaving that meeting, I think a lot of people had visions of Jimmy Carter in their heads," Blinken told

Bergen in reference to the failed attempt by the Carter administration in 1980 to rescue the Americans held hostage at the U.S. embassy in Iran.

John Brennan, Assistant to the President for Homeland Security and Counterterrorism

White House counter-terrorism adviser John Brennan recently told an audience at NYPD [New York Police Department] headquarters in New York that once Obama made the "gutsy call" to approve the mission, "the minutes passed like hours and days."

When an NYPD official asked Brennan what it was like to be at the White House that evening, Brennan said there "wasn't a sense of exuberance, there were no high fives," he said. "People let out a breath. It was a moment of reflection. This was something we'd all worked toward for a long time."

Brennan recalled leaving the White House at 1:30 A.M. and passing by Lafayette Park, where many people had gathered and were chanting, "USA, USA." Brennan said he was hit by a wave of emotion. "I had goose bumps," he said.

James Clapper, Director of National Intelligence

Clapper told [CNN blog] Security Clearance "the tension in the air was palpable," particularly when the helicopter encountered its problem. "There was a lot of tension, and then as it became clear that we were reasonably sure that yes, it was Usama bin Laden, there was, if I can use the phrase, not only emotional closure, but functional closure in that operation illustrated the effectiveness of what an integrated intelligence and operational community could accomplish," he said.

Clapper told Security Clearance he walked with the President through the Rose Garden on their way to the

East Room where Obama addressed the nation. It was the first time they had been outdoors for 12 hours, and they could hear the crowds in Lafayette Park. "It was then that it hit me what a momentous event this was, and I'll not forget that," Clapper said.

"It is hard for me to recall a single vignette that carried with it so much importance, and so much symbolism for this country," Clapper said. "As an intelligence professional that has spent 50 years in the business, I cannot remember an event that would approach that raid and its success in my memory."

Hillary Clinton, Secretary of State

For Secretary Clinton, who was a U.S. Senator from New York on 9/11, the operation provided a sense of closure to her she said recently in an address at the U.S. Naval Academy in Annapolis. "We did our very best to try to give the president our honest assessment, and ultimately you know it was his decision which I fully supported because I believed that we had to take the risk and it was a risk."

"It was a pretty intense, tense, stressful time because the people who were actually doing it on the ground were thousands of miles away," she said. "I'm not sure anyone breathed for you know 35 or 37 minutes."

> 'Everyone was particularly focused on just trying to keep calm and keep prepared as to what would happen.'

"I wasn't even aware people were taking pictures, the White House photographer obviously was, but you were just so concentrating on what you could see and you could hear. We could see or hear nothing when [the SEALs] went into the house. There was no communication or feedback coming so it was during that time period everyone was particularly focused on just trying to keep calm and keep prepared as to what would happen," Clinton said.

William Daley, White House Chief of Staff

President Obama's former chief of staff might have come closest to tipping off the press that something monumental was in the works before Obama made his historic address to the nation.

That Saturday evening, Obama, Daley, and many other senior administration officials were attending the annual White House Correspondents Association dinner in Washington. George Stephanopoulos of ABC News had heard from someone that the White House had uncharacteristically closed itself to public tours the next morning. "You guys have something big going on over there?" Bergen writes of Stephanopoulos's surprising query to Daley. "Oh no. It's just a plumbing issue," Daley said, seemingly ending the newsman's curiosity.

In an address to a conference of public relations executives in Chicago last week, Daley called that night of the operation at the White House the "biggest moment of my life in a professional sense."

Tom Donilon, National Security Adviser

"Well, obviously we're thinking about the successful and safe completion of the mission," Donilon told CNN's Candy Crowley a week after the raid. "That was first and foremost in everybody's mind as we were monitoring the mission as it was ongoing."

"You know, as I look at the picture now though, and focus in on the president, having served three presidents," Donilon told Crowley, "you really are struck by these being quintessentially presidential decisions, and you see it in new experiences that you have."

For Donilon, who watched the president receive divided opinions from his advisers on whether to go forward with the mission, "that's what strikes me now, looking at the president, is that we ask our presidents to make these exceedingly difficult decisions," Donilon said. "And at the end of the day, 300 million Americans are looking to him to make the right decision."

Robert Gates, Secretary of Defense

Gates, who was the only hold over in Obama's cabinet from the previous administration, said for him, the most difficult moment for him that evening was when one of the Blackhawk helicopters carrying a Navy SEALs team crashed in the courtyard of the bin Laden compound.

Like Biden, he was opposed to the operation involving the SEALs. Gates, who spent a majority of his career at the C.I.A. and was the intelligence liaison at the White House in 1980 during the failed attempt to rescue the American hostages held in Iran, advocated for a much larger operation.

> 'My heart went to my mouth when the helicopter landed in the courtyard, 'cause I knew that wasn't part of the plan.'

"Well, I think like the rest, I was just transfixed," Gates told CBS's *60 Minutes* last year. "And of course, my heart went to my mouth when the helicopter landed in the courtyard, 'cause I knew that wasn't part of the plan. But these guys were just amazing."

Admiral Mike Mullen, Chairman of the Joint Chiefs of Staff

For Mullen, there was also a concern about whether the White House would interfere after the helicopter went down.

Mullen told Bergen his biggest concern "was that someone at the White House would reach in and start micromanaging the mission. It is potentially the great disadvantage about technology that we have these days," he said. "And I was going to put my body in the way of trying to stop that. Obviously, there was one person I couldn't stop doing that, and that was the president." . . .

Brigadier General Marshall "Brad" Webb, Assistant Commanding General, Joint Special Operations Command

Webb was the senior officer in the room from Joint Special Operations Command (JSOC). The commanding officer of JSOC, Admiral William McRaven, briefed the officials on the operation from his position in Afghanistan. Webb declined to comment to CNN about his role in the operation, or his reflections of the evening.

Denis McDonough, Deputy National Security Adviser

"I think what strikes me about the picture more than anything is the fact that it speaks to the teamwork that was emblematic," McDonough told CNN's Wolf Blitzer the day after the operation. "The broader teamwork from the IAC, the intelligence community, from the military, from our diplomats, to make sure that this happened in the successful way that it did."

Leon Panetta, Central Intelligence Agency Director

Panetta, who at that point was the Director of the C.I.A. was at the agency headquarters in Langley, VA that evening, but was communicating with Obama and his team via a video link. The Title 50 operation called for the C.I.A. to have operational control, so everyone at the White House was listening to Panetta narrate what was happening.

"There were a number of tense moments going through the operation," now Defense Secretary Panetta said on his way back to the United States from South America last week. "Just the fact that having these helicopters going 150 miles into Pakistan, and the concern about whether or not they would be

> 'There were a number of tense moments going through the operation.'

detected." When one of the helicopters went down at the compound, Panetta said it was "pretty nerve-wracking for a lot of us that, you know, trying to figure out what happens now."

When they received confirmation from the SEAL team that they had killed bin Laden, Panetta said there was a "huge sigh of relief by everybody involved." But with a disabled helicopter down at the compound, it had to be destroyed by members of the team before they were able to leave Pakistani territory. "And so there was a lot of concern about the ability to get everybody back to Afghanistan," Panetta said. "But we were able to do that, and it was at that point that I think everybody kind of looked at everybody and said, 'mission accomplished.'"

1957   March 10: Osama bin Muhammad bin Awad bin Laden is born in Riyadh, Saudi Arabia, the seventeenth of fifty-four children of the billionaire owner of a construction company. He is raised a devout Muslim.

1969   Bin Laden's father dies in a helicopter crash. Bin Laden inherits a reported $80 million.

1979   After graduating from college, Bin Laden moves to Afghanistan to join the jihad against the Soviets occupying the country. He supplies construction equipment, raises money, offers logistical and humanitarian aid, and personally fights.

1988   Bin Laden and several other Islamic leaders form al Qaeda ("the base" in Arabic), a militant Islamist organization.

1989   The Soviet Union withdraws from Afghanistan. Bin Laden returns to Saudi Arabia.

1990   After Iraq invades Kuwait, the Saudi government allows US troops into Saudi Arabia to monitor Iraqi forces. Bin Laden is outraged at the US presence near Muslim holy sites.

1991   The United States drives Iraqi forces from Kuwait (the Gulf War). The Saudi government expels Bin Laden for his continued criticism of the regime. He relocates to Sudan and continues building his terror network.

1992   Al Qaeda executes its first bombing attack against US travelers in a Yemen hotel.

1993   Ramzi Yousef—nephew of Khalid Sheikh Mohammed, who would become the mastermind of the 9/11 attacks—drives a truck bomb below the World Trade Center, killing six people. Bin Laden is not indicted for the attack.

Somali troops associated with al Qaeda shoot down US Black Hawk helicopters, killing eighteen American soldiers.

1994   The government of Saudi Arabia revokes Bin Laden's citizenship and freezes his assets. Bin Laden's family disowns him.

1996   According to several sources, Bin Laden engineers an attempt in the Philippines to assassinate US president Bill Clinton.

Bin Laden issues a fatwa (religious proclamation) against the United States, "Declaration of War Against the Americans Occupying the Land of Two Holy Places." It calls on Muslims to push US forces out of the Holy Land and defeat the enemy.

Sudan expels Bin Laden. He chooses to return to Afghanistan, where he runs training camps for the mujahideens and supplies fighters, arms, and cash.

1998   February 23: Bin Laden issues a fatwa titled "Jihad Against Jews and Crusaders." It states, "The ruling to kill the Americans and their allies—civilians and military—is an individual duty for every Muslim who can do it in any country in which it is possible to do it."

August 7: Truck bombs explode simultaneously outside the US embassies in Nairobi, Kenya, and Dar es Salaam, Tanzania, killing 224 people. The United States indicts Bin Laden on 224 counts of murder. He is put on the FBI's 10 Most Wanted List.

August 20: US Navy ships launch a missile attack on Bin Laden's training camps but miss him.

1999   A CIA plan to capture or kill Bin Laden using Pakistani commandos is aborted after the Pakistani government is ousted by a military coup.

In December, al Qaeda plans New Year's Day attacks on four sites in Jordan; Los Angeles International Airport (LAX); and the USS *The Sullivans*. The Jordan and LAX attacks are foiled by authorities, and the bomb-laden boat headed for *The Sullivans* sinks before reaching it.

2000   October: Al Qaeda suicide bombers attack the US destroyer USS *Cole* in Yemen, killing seventeen soldiers.

2001   September 11: Al Qaeda terrorists hijack four American planes. Two crash into New York City's World Trade Center towers, one into the Pentagon, and one into a field in Pennsylvania after passengers overcome the hijackers. Nearly three thousand people die.

September 20: President George W. Bush asks the Taliban regime in Afghanistan to turn over Bin Laden. The Taliban refuses.

October 7: US and British forces invade Afghanistan.

November–December: US troops and allies attack al Qaeda forces at Tora Bora, a cave complex in the mountains of Afghanistan where they suspect Bin Laden is hiding. They take the compound but do not find Bin Laden.

2002   Terrorist attacks linked to or inspired by al Qaeda claim the lives of more than three hundred people in Pakistan, Peru, Tunisia, Yemen, Kuwait, Indonesia, Jordan, and Kenya.

2003   Terrorist attacks in Saudi Arabia, Morocco, Afghanistan, Indonesia, and Turkey kill nearly two hundred people.

March 1: The mastermind of the 9/11 attacks, al Qaeda's Khalid Sheikh Mohammed, is captured in Pakistan.

2004   Terrorist attacks kill almost two hundred people in Spain, more than one hundred in the Philippines, and forty in Moscow. The Spain attack is linked to al Qaeda.

2005   Fifty-six people are killed and seven hundred injured in an al Qaeda attack in London.

Bin Laden moves to Abbottabad, Pakistan, according to information given by his wives after his death.

2007   US officials learn the name of the courier who would lead to Bin Laden.

Pakistani prime minister Benazir Bhutto is assassinated; an al Qaeda commander claims responsibility.

2009   Officials discover the courier lives in Abbottabad.

2010   Officials discover the compound where they suspect Bin Laden is hiding.

2011   March 14: President Barack Obama and the National Security Council begin meetings about an operation targeting Bin Laden. Options include a bomb strike against the compound, a small targeted missile attack on Bin Laden, or a Navy SEAL raid on the compound.

April 29: President Obama authorizes the SEAL option.

May 1: SEALs take helicopters from Afghanistan into Pakistan and raid the Abbottabad compound, killing Bin Laden, one of his adult sons, and four others. No US troops are hurt. Bin Laden is buried at sea within twenty-four hours.

May 6: Al Qaeda confirms Osama bin Laden's death.

June 21: Pakistan convenes a commission to investigate the details of Bin Laden's death.

2013 January 4: The Abbottabad Commission releases a 336-page report finding that Pakistan's failure to detect Bin Laden's presence showed gross negligence, incompetence, and irresponsibility. However, the commission does not claim that officials knew of Bin Laden's presence or deliberately hid him.

FOR FURTHER READING

Books

Abdel Bari Atwan, *After bin Laden: Al Qaeda, the Next Generation*. London: Saqi Books, 2012.

Peter Bergen, *Holy War, Inc.: Inside the Secret World of Osama bin Laden*. New York: Free Press, 2001.

Peter Bergen, *The Longest War: The Enduring Conflict Between America and Al-Qaeda*. New York: Free Press, 2011.

Peter Bergen, *Manhunt: The Ten-Year Search for Bin Laden from 9/11 to Abbottabad*. New York: Crown, 2012.

Peter Bergen, *The Osama bin Laden I Know: An Oral History of al Qaeda's Leader*. New York: Free Press, 2006.

Najwa bin Laden, Omar bin Laden, and Jean Sasson, *Growing Up bin Laden: Osama's Wife and Son Take Us Inside Their Secret World*. New York: St. Martin's, 2009.

Osama bin Laden, *Messages to the World: The Statements of Osama bin Laden*. New York: Verso, 2005.

Mark Bowden, *The Finish: The Killing of Osama bin Laden*. New York: Atlantic Monthly Press, 2012.

Jason Burke, *Al Qaeda: The True Story of Radical Islam*. London: Tauris, 2004.

David Cole, ed., *The Torture Memos: Rationalizing the Unthinkable*. New York: The New Press, 2009.

Dalton Fury, *Kill bin Laden: A Delta Force Commander's Account of the Hunt for the World's Most Wanted Man*. New York: St. Martin's, 2008.

Robert Gates, *Duty: Memoirs of a Secretary at War*. New York: Knopf, 2014.

Fawaz A. Gerges, *The Rise and Fall of Al-Qaeda*. New York: Oxford University Press, 2011.

Terry McDermott and Josh Meyer, *The Hunt for KSM: Inside the Pursuit and Takedown of the Real 9/11 Mastermind, Khalid Sheikh Mohammed*. New York: Back Bay Books, 2012.

Mark Owen and Kevin Maurer, *No Easy Day: The Autobiography of a Navy Seal*. New York: Dutton, 2012.

Chuck Pfarrer, *Seal Target Geronimo*. New York: St. Martin's, 2012.

Ali H. Soufan, *The Black Banners: The Inside Story of 9/11 and the War Against al-Qaeda*. New York: Norton, 2011.

Lawrence Wright, *The Looming Tower: Al Qaeda and the Road to 9/11*. New York: Vintage, 2006.

Periodicals and Internet Sources

Matthew Alexander, "Tortured Logic," *Foreign Policy*, May 4, 2011. www.foreignpolicy.com.

Abdulaziz Alhiez and Hamza Mustafa, "Al Qaeda: The Third Generation? Parts 1 and 2," Al Jazeera, February 26 and February 28, 2014. www.aljazeera.com.

Abdulrahman al-Masri, Michele Chabin, Mona Alami, and Sarah Lynch, "Al-Qaeda Influence Spreads Unchecked," *USA Today*, January 8, 2014.

Associated Press, "Senate Report: Torture Didn't Lead to bin Laden," *Washington Post*, March 31, 2014. www.washington post.com.

Peter Bergen, "From bin Laden to Boston," CNN, April 30, 2013. www.cnn.com.

Peter Bergen, "The Battle for Tora Bora," *New Republic*, December 22, 2009. www.newrepublic.com.

Mark Bowden, "The Hunt for Geronimo," *Vanity Fair*, November 2012. www.vanityfair.com.

Steve Coll, "Disturbing and Misleading" (Review of *Zero Dark Thirty*), *New York Review of Books*, February 7, 2013.

"Death of Osama Bin Laden Fast Facts," CNN Library, September 9, 2013. www.cnn.com.

Yochi Dreazen, "Bin Laden Documents Offer Different Picture of Terrorist Leader," *National Journal*, May 3, 2012.

Carlotta Gall, "What Pakistan Knew About bin Laden," *New York Times*, March 19, 2014. www.nytimes.com.

Jeff Greenfield, "What If bin Laden Had Been Captured, Not Killed? An Alternate History," *Washington Post*, May 6, 2011. www.washingtonpost.com.

Alexis Madrigal, "Outside the White House, a Celebration of bin Laden's Death," *The Atlantic*, May 2, 2011. www.theatlantic.com.

Ron Moreau and Sami Yousafzai, "Osama Was My Neighbor," *Daily Beast*, May 2, 2011. www.thedailybeast.com.

Brendan O'Neill, "How the West Was Won over by a Hit for a Falling Star," *The Australian*, May 7, 2011. www.theaustralian.com.au.

"Osama bin Laden's Death: How It Happened," BBC News, September 10, 2012. www.bbc.com.

Bill Roggio and Thomas Joscelyn, "Strategic Retreat," *Weekly Standard*, February 6, 2012. www.weeklystandard.com.

Olivier Roy, "Leader of Loners and Outcasts," *New Statesman*, May 9, 2011.

"The Zero Dark Thirty File: Lifting the Government's Shroud over the Mission That Killed Osama bin Laden," National Security Archive, January 17, 2013. www2.gwu.edu.

Websites

In Depth: The Killing of Osama bin Laden (www.cbsnews.com/feature/the-killing-of-osama-bin-laden). This CBS news website provides access to the network's multimedia coverage of the Navy SEAL raid in Pakistan and links to recent news articles on related topics.

Islamic Fundamentalism (www.huffingtonpost.com/tag/islamic-fundamentalism). This *Huffington Post* portal provides links to a wealth of stories related to the topic of Islamic fundamentalism, including Osama bin Laden's assassination, 9/11, al Qaeda, and other Islamic terrorist groups.

Osama bin Laden: 9/11 Mastermind Is Dead (http://content .time.com/time/specials/packages/0,28757,2068895,00.html). This *Time* magazine portal provides access to dozens of the magazine's articles and videos on Osama bin Laden, al Qaeda, and 9/11, including the latest headlines.

INDEX

183

36-36   7/14/15.